FOOD&WINE
COCKTAILS
2015

FOOD & WINE COCKTAILS 2015
EDITOR IN CHIEF **Dana Cowin**
EXECUTIVE EDITOR **Kate Krader**
CHIEF MIXOLOGIST **John deBary**
EDITOR **Susan Choung**
COPY EDITOR **Lisa Leventer**
EDITORIAL ASSISTANT **Manon Cooper**
RESEARCHER **Jennifer Salerno**
ADDITIONAL RESEARCH BY **Chelsea Morse**

DESIGNER **Phoebe Flynn Rich**
PRODUCTION DIRECTOR **Joseph Colucci**
PRODUCTION MANAGER **Stephanie Thompson**

PHOTOGRAPHER **Lucas Allen**
STYLIST **Lee Blaylock**
ILLUSTRATOR **Ben Wiseman**

ON THE COVER **Blood and Sand (left), p. 148,
and The Yubari King, p. 125**

TIME HOME ENTERTAINMENT
PUBLISHER **Margot Schupf**
VICE PRESIDENT, FINANCE **Vandana Patel**
EXECUTIVE DIRECTOR, MARKETING SERVICES
  Carol Pittard
EXECUTIVE DIRECTOR, BUSINESS DEVELOPMENT
  Suzanne Albert
EXECUTIVE DIRECTOR, MARKETING
  Susan Hettleman
ASSISTANT DIRECTOR OF DIRECT MARKETING
  Kristy Harrison
ASSISTANT GENERAL COUNSEL **Simone Procas**
SENIOR PRODUCTION MANAGER
  Susan Chodakiewicz
ASSISTANT PROJECT MANAGER **Allyson Angle**

FOOD & WINE MAGAZINE
SVP/EDITOR IN CHIEF **Dana Cowin**
CREATIVE DIRECTOR **Fredrika Stjärne**
EXECUTIVE MANAGING EDITOR **Mary Ellen Ward**
EXECUTIVE EDITOR **Pamela Kaufman**
DEPUTY EDITOR **Christine Quinlan**
EXECUTIVE FOOD EDITOR **Tina Ujlaki**
EXECUTIVE WINE EDITOR **Ray Isle**
DIGITAL DIRECTOR **Alex Vallis**

FEATURES
RESTAURANT EDITOR **Kate Krader**
DEPUTY WINE EDITOR **Megan Krigbaum**
STYLE EDITOR **Suzie Myers**
ASSOCIATE EDITORS **Chelsea Morse,
  M. Elizabeth Sheldon**
ASSISTANT EDITOR **Maren Ellingboe**

FOOD
DEPUTY EDITOR **Kate Heddings**
SENIOR EDITOR **Sarah DiGregorio**
TEST KITCHEN SENIOR EDITORS
  Justin Chapple, Kay Chun
ASSOCIATE EDITOR **Ben Mims**
EDITORIAL ASSISTANT **Julia Heffelfinger**
TEST KITCHEN ASSISTANT **Emily Tylman**

ART
ART DIRECTOR **James Maikowski**
SENIOR DESIGNER **Angelica Domingo**
DESIGNER **Bianca Jackson**

PHOTO
PHOTO EDITOR **Sara Parks**
ASSOCIATE PHOTO EDITOR **Samantha Bolton**
PHOTO ASSISTANT **Olivia Weiner**

COPY & RESEARCH
COPY CHIEF **Elizabeth Herr**
SENIOR EDITOR **Amanda Woytus**
ASSOCIATE RESEARCH EDITOR
  Erin Laverty Healy

PRODUCTION
DIRECTOR **Joseph Colucci**

DIGITAL MEDIA
DEPUTY DIGITAL EDITOR **Lawrence Marcus**
ASSOCIATE DIGITAL EDITORS
  Noah Kaufman, Justine Sterling
EDITORIAL ASSISTANT **Brianna Wippman**
SENIOR PRODUCER **Caitlin Drexler**
PHOTO COORDINATOR **Erin Fagerland**

ASSOCIATE MANAGING EDITOR **Kerianne Hansen**

TRAVEL CORRESPONDENT **Jennifer Flowers**

ASSISTANT TO THE EDITOR IN CHIEF
  Annie P. Quigley

FOOD&WINE
COCKTAILS
2015

FOOD&WINE
BOOKS
Time Inc. Affluent Media Group, New York

POUR MA GUEULE, P. 72

CONTENTS

FLAVOR KEY

These symbols tell what to expect in each drink.

● **STRONG** *High alcohol content by volume*

● **SWEET** *Simple syrup, honey, sweet liqueurs or mixers*

● **TART** *Lemon, lime or other citrus*

● **BITTER** *Bitters, Campari or other bitter liqueurs*

● **FRUITY** *Berries, melons, other fruit or fruit-based liqueurs*

● **HERBAL** *Herbs, Chartreuse or other herbal liqueurs*

● **SMOKY** *Mezcal, peated Scotch or other smoky ingredients*

● **SPICY** *Chiles, cayenne, ginger or other hot ingredients*

FOREWORD

Since we launched *F&W Cocktails* 11 years ago, we've watched many of the mixologists we've highlighted become superstars. So much so that this year, we are dedicating the entire book to 25 up-and-coming talents. They are men and women with diverse backgrounds (one was an artist, another a champion barista) and strong points of view. Ryan Casey, for instance, seasons ice cubes with smoked paprika for his complex, bourbon-based Sergio Leone (p. 126); Karen Grill is a master of perfectly balanced, minimalist cocktails like the four-ingredient rye Nightcap (p. 168). We're proud to share drinks from all 25 of these exceptional mixologists—a taste of the future.

Editor in Chief
FOOD & WINE Magazine

Executive Editor
FOOD & WINE Cocktails

GLASSWARE

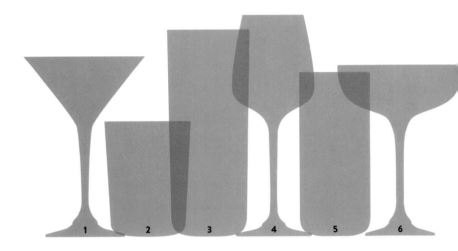

1 MARTINI

A stemmed glass with a cone-shaped bowl for cocktails served straight up (mixed with ice and then strained).

2 ROCKS

A short, wide-mouthed glass for spirits served neat (without ice) and cocktails poured over ice. **Single rocks** glasses hold up to 6 ounces; **double rocks** glasses hold closer to 12 ounces.

3 COLLINS

A very tall, narrow glass often used for drinks that are served on ice and topped with soda.

4 WINEGLASS

A tall, slightly rounded, stemmed glass for wine-based cocktails. White wine glasses are a fine substitute for highball glasses and are also good for frozen drinks. Balloon-shaped red wine glasses are ideal for fruity cocktails as well as punches.

5 HIGHBALL

A tall, narrow glass that helps preserve the fizz in cocktails that are served with ice and topped with sparkling beverages such as club soda, tonic water or ginger beer.

6 COUPE

A shallow, wide-mouthed, stemmed glass primarily for small (short) and potent cocktails that are served straight up.

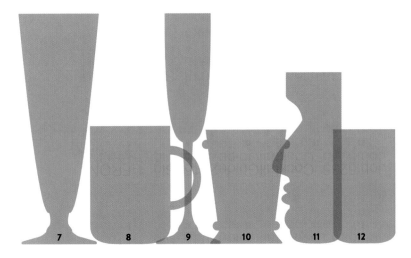

7 PILSNER

A tall, flared glass designed for beer. It's also good for serving oversize cocktails on ice or drinks with multiple garnishes.

8 HEATPROOF GLASS OR MUG

A durable ceramic or glass cup with a handle. Perfect for coffee spiked with whiskey or other spirits as well as toddies and other hot drinks.

9 FLUTE

A tall, slender, usually stemmed glass; its narrow shape helps keep cocktails topped with Champagne or sparkling wine effervescent.

10 JULEP CUP

A short pewter or silver cup designed to keep juleps (minty, crushed-ice cocktails) cold.

11 TIKI MUG

A tall ceramic mug without a handle that's decorated with a Polynesian-style or tropical motif. It's designed specifically for tiki drinks.

12 FIZZ

A narrow glass for soda-topped drinks without ice. Also called a juice glass or Delmonico glass.

BAR TOOLS

1 HAWTHORNE STRAINER

The best all-purpose strainer. A semicircular spring ensures a spill-proof fit on a shaker. Look for a tightly coiled spring, which keeps muddled fruit and herbs out of drinks.

2 JIGGER

A two-sided stainless steel measuring instrument for precise mixing. Look for double-sided ones with ½- and ¾-ounce and 1- and 2-ounce cups. A shot glass with measures works, too.

3 MUDDLER

A sturdy tool that's used to crush herbs, sugar cubes and fresh fruit; it's traditionally made of wood. Choose a muddler that can reach the bottom of a cocktail shaker; in a pinch, substitute a long-handled wooden spoon.

4 CHANNEL KNIFE

A small, spoon-shaped knife with a metal tooth. Creates garnishes by turning citrus-fruit peels into long, thin spiral-cut twists (see Making a Twist, p. 26).

5 JULEP STRAINER

The preferred device for straining cocktails from a mixing glass because it fits securely. Fine holes keep ice out of the drink.

6 CITRUS JUICER

A metal or ceramic citrus press, available in a variety of sizes, that allows you to squeeze lemons, limes and oranges *à la minute*.

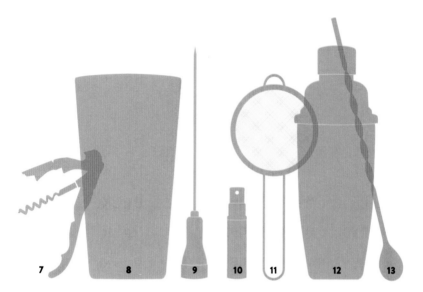

7 WAITER'S CORKSCREW

A pocketknife-like tool with an attached bottle opener. Bartenders prefer it to bulkier, more complicated corkscrews.

---

8 BOSTON SHAKER

The bartender's choice; consists of a mixing glass, usually a pint glass, with a metal canister that covers the glass to create a seal. Shake drinks with the metal half pointing away from you. Alternatively, replace the mixing glass with a small shaking tin.

9 ICE PICK

A sharp metal tool with a sturdy handle used to break off chunks from a larger block of ice.

---

10 ATOMIZER

A small spray bottle used to disperse tiny quantities of aromatic liquid evenly over the surface of an empty glass or on top of a cocktail. Atomizers are widely available at drugstores.

---

11 FINE STRAINER

A fine-mesh strainer set over a glass before the cocktail is poured in (see Fine-Straining Drinks, p. 27). It keeps bits of muddled herbs, fruit and crushed ice out of drinks.

---

12 COBBLER SHAKER

A shaker with a metal cup for mixing drinks with ice, a built-in strainer and a fitted top.

---

13 BAR SPOON

A long-handled metal spoon that mixes cocktails without creating air bubbles. Also useful for measuring small amounts of liquid.

ESSENTIAL SPIRITS

Mixologists will use just about anything they can get their hands on, but these spirits are still the backbone of a great cocktail list.

VODKA

Produced all over the world, vodka is traditionally distilled from fermented grain or potatoes, but nearly any fruit or vegetable can be used, from grapes to beets. Most **flavored** vodkas are created by adding ingredients to a neutral spirit; the best macerate citrus, berries or herbs in high-proof alcohol.

GIN

Gin is made by distilling a neutral grain spirit with botanicals such as juniper, coriander and citrus peels. The most ubiquitous style is **London dry,** *above.* **Plymouth** gin is less dry and juniper-forward, while **Old Tom** gin is slightly sweeter than London dry. **New Western** gins, such as Hendrick's, incorporate unusual botanicals like rose petals. **Genever,** a predecessor to gin, is a botanically rich, malted grain–based spirit. **Aquavit,** like gin, is made from a neutral alcohol and botanicals such as caraway, citrus peels and star anise.

TEQUILA

Authentic tequila is made from 100 percent blue agave that is harvested by hand, slow-roasted in ovens, fermented, then distilled. **Blanco** (white) tequila is unaged. **Reposado** (rested) tequila, *above*, ages up to one year in barrels. **Añejo** (aged) tequila must be matured between one and three years. **Mezcal** is known for its smoky flavor, which comes from roasting the agave in earthen pits; the finest mezcals are unaged. **Sotol** is a grassy, vegetal mezcal relative made from an agave-like plant called desert spoon (*sotol* in Spanish).

RUM

Distilled from sugarcane or its residues, rums are typically produced in tropical regions. **White,** a.k.a. silver or light, rum can be aged, then filtered to remove color. **Amber** (or gold) rum, *above*, is often aged in barrels for a short time; caramel is sometimes added for color. **Dark** rums, made with molasses, include **blackstrap** rum, a rich, thick variety produced from blackstrap molasses; and **Demerara** rum, made on the banks of Guyana's Demerara River, with a burnt-sugar flavor. **Rhum agricole** and **cachaça** are distilled from fresh sugarcane juice.

WHISKEY

Whiskey is distilled from a fermented mash of grains, then typically matured in oak barrels. Scotland and Japan are famous for their **single malts** (produced from 100 percent malted barley from one distillery). **Highland Scotches** are single malts of various styles from Scotland's Highland area. Most **peated** whisky comes from Islay in Scotland. Canada favors **blended** whiskies high in rye. America is known for its **bourbon**, robust **rye** and unaged **white** whiskeys. **Irish** whiskeys tend to be mellow blends.

BRANDY

Brandies are distilled from a fermented mash of fruit. French grape brandies like **Armagnac** and **Cognac,** *above,* are named for the regions where they are made. **Calvados** is brandy made from apples (and sometimes pears) in the Normandy region of France. **Applejack** is an American apple brandy blended with neutral spirits. Other styles include **pisco,** distilled from aromatic grapes in Peru and Chile; and **eau-de-vie,** a specialty of the European Alps, distilled from a fermented fruit mash and bottled without aging.

APERITIFS (wine-based)

The word *aperitif* is often used to refer to any pre-dinner drink, but aperitifs are also a category of beverage: light, dry and low-proof, with characteristic bitter flavors. A century ago, mixologists began adding wine-based aperitifs to cocktails instead of simply serving them on their own before meals. Wine-based aperitifs include **quinquinas** (or kinas); these contain quinine, a bitter extract from cinnamon-like cinchona bark. Some well-known examples are Lillet, *above,* and Dubonnet.

APERITIFS (spirit-based)

Low-proof, bitter spirit-based aperitifs like **Campari,** *above,* have always been popular in Europe. Now they're beloved in the US thanks to mixologists' embrace of bottles like **Aperol,** the bitter orange Italian aperitivo. Other examples of spirit-based aperitifs are **Pimm's No. 1,** a gin-based English aperitif with subtle spice and citrus flavors; and **Cynar,** which is made from 13 herbs and plants, including artichokes.

VERMOUTH

Vermouth is an aromatic fortified wine flavored with botanicals. **Dry** vermouth, *above,* is a staple in martinis. **Sweet** vermouth, which is red, is best known as whiskey's partner in a Manhattan. Italian **bianco** and French **blanc** represent another style that's slightly sweeter than dry vermouth; **rosé** and **rosato** vermouths are pink, with a spicy flavor. **Cocchi Vermouth di Torino** is an Italian red vermouth that's drier and more complex than other red vermouths.

AMARO

Amaros ("bitters" in Italian) are bittersweet sipping spirits made by infusing or distilling a neutral spirit with herbs, spices, citrus peels or nuts before sweetening and bottling. Traditionally served after dinner to aid digestion, amaros like Averna, Montenegro and Nonino, *above,* are popular with American bartenders for the complexity and balance they add to cocktails.

LIQUEURS

Among the oldest spirits, liqueurs are produced from a base alcohol that's distilled or macerated with a variety of ingredients, then sweetened. Sugar makes up to 35 percent of a liqueur's weight by volume, and up to 40 percent for **crème liqueurs** such as crème de menthe. Liqueurs can be herbal **(Chartreuse)**; citrus- or fruit-based **(Cointreau)**; floral (violet-inflected **parfait amour,** *above*); or nut- or seed-based (**nocino**, made from unripe green walnuts).

BASIC BAR

The essentials you need to make cocktails like Moscow Mules, old-fashioneds and margaritas.

Stock your bar cart with the items called out below.

BOTTLES	TOOLS	GLASSES
Vodka	**Shaker**	**Double rocks glasses**
London dry gin	**Mixing glass**	**Collins glasses**
Bourbon	**Jiggers (¹/₂ & ³/₄ oz. and 1 & 2 oz.)**	**Wineglasses***
Dark rum	**Hawthorne strainer**	**Heatproof mugs***
Blanco tequila	**Bar spoon**	Small and large coupes
Orange liqueur/ triple sec	**Corkscrew**	Fizz glasses
Angostura bitters	**Fine strainer**	Martini glasses
Scotch	Ice pick	Pilsners
Cognac	Large ice cube molds	Julep cups
White rum	Muddler	Champagne flutes
Rye whiskey	Citrus juicer	Highball glasses
Irish whiskey	Atomizer	Tiki mugs
Absinthe	Flask	
Dry vermouth	Apron	
Sweet vermouth	Thermos	
Peychaud's bitters	Channel knife	
Flavored vodka	Microplane	
Pisco	iSi canister	
New Western gin		
Herbal liqueurs such as Chartreuse, Bénédictine, etc.		
Fruit eau-de-vie		
Gentian aperitif/ liqueur such as Suze		
Amaro		
Orange bitters		
Celery bitters		*not pictured

STEPPED-UP BAR

Serious and funky spirits, glassware for drinks served straight up, plus a pick to carve ice like a mixologist.

Stock your bar cart with the items called out below.

BOTTLES	TOOLS	GLASSES
Vodka	Shaker	Double rocks glasses
London dry gin	Mixing glass	Collins glasses
Bourbon	Jiggers (½ & ¾ oz.	Wineglasses*
Dark rum	and 1 & 2 oz.)	Heatproof mugs*
Blanco tequila	Hawthorne strainer	Small and large
Orange liqueur/	Bar spoon	coupes
triple sec	Corkscrew	Fizz glasses
Angostura bitters	Fine strainer	Martini glasses*
Scotch	Ice pick	Pilsners*
Cognac	Large ice cube molds	Julep cups
White rum	Muddler	Champagne flutes
Rye whiskey	Citrus juicer	Highball glasses
Irish whiskey	Atomizer	Tiki mugs
Absinthe	Flask	
Dry vermouth	Apron	
Sweet vermouth	Thermos	
Peychaud's bitters	Channel knife	
Flavored vodka	Microplane	
Pisco	iSi canister	
New Western gin		
Herbal liqueurs		
such as Chartreuse,		
Bénédictine, etc.		
Fruit eau-de-vie		
Gentian aperitif/		
liqueur such as Suze		
Amaro		
Orange bitters		
Celery bitters		

*not pictured

PRO-STYLE BAR

A range of complex spirits with herbal and bitter flavors, plus an iSi charger for carbonated drinks and an atomizer for misting.

Stock your bar cart with all of these items.

BOTTLES

Vodka
London dry gin
Bourbon
Dark rum
Blanco tequila
Orange liqueur/
triple sec
Angostura bitters
Scotch
Cognac
White rum
Rye whiskey
Irish whiskey
Absinthe
Dry vermouth
Sweet vermouth
Peychaud's bitters
Flavored vodka
Pisco
New Western gin
Herbal liqueurs
such as Chartreuse,
Bénédictine, etc.
Fruit eau-de-vie
Gentian aperitif/
liqueur such as Suze
Amaro
Orange bitters
Celery bitters

TOOLS

Shaker
Mixing glass
Jiggers (½ & ¾ oz.
and 1 & 2 oz.)
Hawthorne strainer
Bar spoon
Corkscrew
Fine strainer
Ice pick
Large ice cube molds
Muddler
Citrus juicer
Atomizer
Flask
Apron
Thermos
Channel knife
Microplane
iSi canister

GLASSES

Double rocks glasses
Collins glasses
Wineglasses*
Heatproof mugs*
Small and large
coupes
Fizz glasses
Martini glasses*
Pilsners*
Julep cups
Champagne flutes
Highball glasses*
Tiki mugs*

*not pictured

BAR LEXICON

ABSINTHE An herbal spirit, formerly banned in the US, flavored with botanicals such as wormwood, green anise and fennel seeds.

ALLSPICE DRAM Also known as pimento dram; a rum-based liqueur infused with Jamaican allspice berries.

APEROL A vibrant orange-red aperitivo flavored with bitter orange, rhubarb, gentian and cinchona bark.

APPLEJACK An American apple brandy blended with neutral spirits.

BATAVIA-ARRACK VAN OOSTEN (left) A clear, spicy and citrusy rum-like spirit made in Java from sugarcane and fermented red rice.

BÉNÉDICTINE An herbal liqueur with flavors of hyssop, angelica, juniper and myrrh. According to legend, the recipe was developed by a French monk in 1510.

BITTERS A concentrated tincture of bitter and aromatic herbs, roots and spices that adds complexity to drinks. Varieties include orange, chocolate and aromatic bitters, the best known of which is **Angostura**. **Bittermens** makes bitters in unusual flavors like Elemakule Tiki. **Peychaud's** bitters have flavors of anise and cherry.

BONAL GENTIANE-QUINA A slightly bitter French aperitif wine infused with gentian root and cinchona bark, the source of quinine.

BONDED A term used for a single-distillery-produced liquor (such as whiskey or apple brandy) that's distilled during a single season, aged at least four years, bottled at 100 proof and stored in a "bonded" warehouse under US government supervision.

CAMPARI A potent, bright red aperitivo with a bitter orange flavor. It's made from a secret blend of fruit, herbs and spices.

CARPANO ANTICA FORMULA A rich and complex sweet red vermouth from Italy.

CHARTREUSE A spicy herbal French liqueur made from more than 100 botanicals; **green** Chartreuse is more potent than the honey-sweetened **yellow** one.

COCCHI AMERICANO A low-alcohol, white-wine-based aperitivo infused with cinchona bark, citrus peels and herbs such as gentian. The **rosa** variety is more bitter and aromatic than the **white.**

COCCHI VERMOUTH DI TORINO A slightly bitter, Moscato-based red vermouth from Italy with hints of citrus, rhubarb and cocoa.

COINTREAU A French triple sec that is made by macerating and distilling sun-dried sweet and bitter orange peels.

COMBIER PAMPLEMOUSSE ROSE (above left) A pale pink liqueur made by infusing ripe red grapefruit in a neutral alcohol.

CREMA DE MEZCAL A creamy, sweet and smoky blend of mezcal (90 percent) and agave nectar (10 percent).

CRÈME DE CACAO A cacao-flavored liqueur that's less sweet than chocolate liqueur. It can be **dark** (brown) or **white** (colorless).

CRÈME DE NOYAUX An almond-flavored crème liqueur made from apricot pit kernels.

CURAÇAO A general term for orange-flavored liqueurs historically produced in the French West Indies.

CYNAR A pleasantly bitter aperitivo made from 13 herbs and plants, including artichokes.

DON'S SPICES #2 A sweet and spicy syrup made with allspice and vanilla; often used in tiki drinks.

GÉNÉPY DES ALPES (left) A pungent herbal liqueur made from Génépy, the same rare Alpine plant used in Chartreuse.

GRAN CLASSICO BITTER A revival of the 1860s Bitter of Turin aperitivo, made from gentian, bitter orange, rhubarb and hyssop, among other ingredients.

GUM SYRUP A simple syrup that's been thickened with gum arabic, made from the sap of acacia trees.

HEERING CHERRY LIQUEUR A crimson-colored cherry liqueur made in Denmark since 1818. Heering is drier and more complex than other cherry liqueurs.

KRONAN SWEDISH PUNSCH A sweet liqueur created from sugarcane spirits including Batavia-Arrack van Oosten (p. 22).

LILLET A wine-based aperitif flavored with orange peel and quinine. The **rouge** variety is sweeter than the **blanc**. The **rosé** (a blend of the red and white) has a slightly fruity flavor.

MARASCHINO LIQUEUR A colorless Italian liqueur. The best brands are distilled from sour marasca cherries and their pits, then aged and sweetened with sugar.

ORGEAT A sweet syrup made from almonds or almond extract and rose or orange flower water.

OVERPROOF RUM Any rum that contains over 60 percent alcohol.

PACHARÁN A Spanish digestif liqueur made from sloe berries, smaller, tart cousins of damson plums.

PASTIS A licorice-flavored French spirit that turns cloudy when mixed with water. It's similar to absinthe (p. 22) but sweeter and lower in alcohol.

PIMM'S NO. 1 A gin-based English aperitif often served with ginger beer, 7-Up or lemonade.

PINEAU DES CHARENTES A barrel-aged French aperitif produced from unfermented grape juice and young Cognac. It can be **white, red** (above) or **rosé**.

PORT A fortified wine from the Douro region of Portugal. Styles include fruity, young **ruby** port and richer, nuttier **tawny**.

PUNT E MES A spicy, orange-accented sweet Italian vermouth fortified with bitters.

ROOT LIQUEUR A digestif made from an infusion of herbs and spices. It is similar in taste to root beer.

SALERS A French gentian root–based aperitif. It has a pronounced bitterness that's balanced by sweetness from white wine and botanicals.

SHERRY A fortified wine from Spain's Jerez region. Varieties include dry styles like **fino** and **manzanilla**; nuttier, richer **amontillado** and **oloroso**; and viscous, sweet **Pedro Ximénez (PX), Moscatel** and **cream** sherry. **East India** sherry falls between an oloroso and a PX in style.

STREGA (left) An Italian liqueur infused with approximately 70 herbs and spices. One of them is saffron, which gives it a golden yellow color.

SUZE A bittersweet, aromatic yellow aperitif made from gentian root with hints of vanilla, candied orange and spice.

TRIPLE SEC An orange-flavored liqueur that is similar to curaçao but not as sweet. **Cointreau,** created in 1875, is the most famous. **Combier,** created in 1834, claims to be the world's first.

VELVET FALERNUM A low-alcohol, sugarcane-based liqueur from Barbados flavored with clove, almond and lime.

VERJUS The pressed, unfermented juice of unripe grapes. It is tart and frequently used in place of vinegar.

VS Cognacs labeled VS (Very Special) are aged at least two years.

SLOE GIN A bittersweet liqueur produced by infusing gin or a neutral spirit with damson plum–like sloe berries and sugar.

SOTOL A Mexican spirit related to mezcal, made from an agave-like plant called desert spoon (*sotol* in Spanish).

ST-GERMAIN A French liqueur created by blending macerated elderflower blossoms with eau-de-vie. It has hints of pear, peach and grapefruit zest.

VSOP Cognacs labeled VSOP (Very Superior Old Pale) must be aged at least four years.

ZUCCA (above) A bittersweet, slightly smoky aperitivo made from rhubarb and flavored with cardamom, citrus and vanilla.

MIXOLOGY BASICS

MAKING A TWIST

A small strip of citrus zest adds concentrated citrus flavor from the peel's essential oils.

A standard twist:

Use a sharp paring knife or peeler to cut a thin, oval disk of the peel, avoiding the pith.

Grasp the twist skin side down and pinch it over the drink. Then either discard, set it on the rim or drop it into the drink.

A spiral-cut twist:

Working over the drink, use a channel knife (p. 10) to cut a 3-inch piece of peel with some pith intact.

Wrap the twist around a straw; tighten at both ends to create a curlicue.

FLAMING A TWIST

Flaming an orange or lemon twist caramelizes its essential oils.

Gently grasp a standard twist, skin side down, between your thumb and two fingers. Hold it about 4 inches over the drink.

Hold a lit match an inch away from the twist–don't let the flame touch the peel–then sharply pinch the twist so the citrus oils fall through the flame and into the drink.

RIMMING A GLASS

Spread salt (preferably kosher), sugar or other powdered ingredient on a small plate.

Moisten half or all of the outer rim of a glass with a citrus-fruit wedge, water or syrup; roll the rim on the plate until it is lightly coated, then tap to release any excess.

THE RIGHT ICE

Big blocks of ice for punch: Pour water into a large, shallow plastic container and freeze. To unmold, let the container sit briefly at room temperature. Alternatively, buy large blocks from local ice purveyors.

Perfect ice cubes: Use flexible silicone ice molds (available from *tovolo.com*) to make precisely square cubes or large cubes for rocks glasses. Or make a large block of ice in a loaf pan and use an ice pick to break off chunks.

Crushed ice: Wrap ice cubes in a clean kitchen towel, then pound them with a wooden mallet or rolling pin.

Cracked ice: Put an ice cube in your hand and tap with the back of a bar spoon until it breaks into pieces.

SMACKING HERBS

Gently clapping fresh herbs between your hands accentuates their aromas and releases essential oils into the drink.

FINE-STRAINING DRINKS

Remove tiny fruit or herb particles to make your drink look cleaner.

Set a fine strainer over a serving glass.

Make your drink in a shaker or mixing glass, set a Hawthorne or julep strainer (p. 10) on top, then pour through both strainers into the serving glass.

25 RISING STAR MIXOLOGISTS

There are so many incredible women and men tending bar these days. Here, we spotlight 25 of the brightest talents, whose exceptional drink recipes appear in this book. These rising stars of the cocktail world are pushing boundaries in so many ways: with unconventional seasonings (cayenne, cilantro), syrups (chai tea) and infusions (pickled-onion vermouth). Here's a look at them and their diverse and far-ranging stories and styles.

CHAD ARNHOLT
The Perennial,
San Francisco

Arnholt's superb Asian-style cocktails helped make Trick Dog a drinks destination in the Bay Area. At his latest venture, The Perennial, he's focused on sustainability: "That means creating drinks using ingredients grown in our own greenhouse, incorporating liqueurs made in the area and buying energy-efficient equipment. It's a gesture, but if someone else likes what they see, they might catch on and want to do the same." *59 Ninth St.; theperennialsf.com.*

NICK BENNETT
Porchlight,
New York City

Trained at his uncle's dive bar in Sag Harbor, Long Island, Bennett mastered molecular tools and techniques at the high-tech Booker and Dax. Now at Porchlight, he's traded in his centrifuge and iSi charger for simple muddlers and bar spoons to create twists on Southern classics. His emphasis on hospitality and bartending technique, however, has stayed with him. "When I want to put the best drink possible in front of a customer, it's the technique that matters most. The ingredients are just the ingredients."
271 11th Ave.;
porchlightnyc.com.

RYAN CASEY
Edmund's Oast,
Charleston, SC

From dives to members-only clubs, Casey has poured drinks in almost every kind of bar. Now at Edmund's Oast, a restaurant known for its impressive list of craft beers, he transforms classic drinks using oddball ingredients like thyme–sweet tea ice cubes. Casey is also fascinated by history and incorporates that knowledge into his recipes: The vinegar in his Charleston Sour, for example, is infused with pineapple–a symbol of hospitality since Colonial days.
1081 Morrison Dr.;
edmundsoast.com.

JACYARA DE OLIVEIRA
Sportsman's Club,
Chicago

De Oliveira discovered her passion for bartending when she lived in Brazil for a year, slinging beers at her then-boyfriend's bar. "*Bar* is actually a loose term for it," she says. "It was an empty space with a cooler full of cold beer, a carton of cigarettes and cachaça." At Sportsman's Club, she helps oversee the tightly curated cocktail list, including a daily changing mixed amaro shot often made with local Letherbee Fernet. *948 N. Western Ave.;*
drinkingandgathering.com.

NICK DETRICH

Cane & Table,
New Orleans

Detrich's résumé includes bartending stints at a strip club and a nightclub. Now at Cane & Table, he's mixing exceptional Caribbean-inspired "proto-tiki" cocktails like the Two Palms (p. 76), made with gin, coconut water and lime. Detrich is also a walking Wikipedia of all things Southern drink-related; for instance, he can tell you about the coconut-and-gin hangover cure that Hemingway drank on Caribbean fishing trips. *1113 Decatur St.; caneandtablenola.com.*

MEGHAN EASTMAN

San Diego

Eastman believes in creating drinks that are approachable but meticulous. At the acclaimed speakeasy Noble Experiment, she specialized in minimalist cocktails. "I don't try to be supershowy," she says, "but I aim for perfection." She's been known to invite guests who were intimidated by the menu to join her behind the bar, where she showed them how to make drinks like the Bitter Scotsman (a mix of Scotch, orgeat, lemon, Campari and cinnamon; p. 136). Eastman, who studied interior architecture, divides her time between guest bartending and her other passion, designing restaurants.

CHRIS ELFORD

Rob Roy, Seattle

A Certified Cicerone (beer professional), Elford also worked as a whiskey distiller, a stand-up comic and a satirical 'zine publisher. After a year of making cocktails at Seattle's famed Canon, he's now at Rob Roy, where he serves pre-Prohibition-era drinks and riffs on classics. He's also passionate about teaching customers—he'll even write down a recipe for them: "I want people to walk away with real knowledge and say, 'Wow! I never knew the difference between a bourbon and a rye Manhattan! Now I know how to make them.'" *2332 Second Ave.; robroyseattle.com.*

KAREN FU

The Happiest Hour,
New York City

Though she learned
bartending basics
at a tiny dive bar after
college, Fu credits
her time with mixology
genius Jim Meehan
at PDT in New York City
as her formative cocktail
experience. She often
builds her greenmarket-
driven drinks around
one fresh ingredient,
like strawberries or
Concord grapes (as
in Deep Purple, Reprise,
p. 48). For her recipes
in this book, Fu visited
bodegas and small liquor
stores: "I tried to be
aware of what the public
has access to without
struggling to find
obscure ingredients
and rare spirits."
121 W. 10th St.;
happiesthournyc.com.

KAREN GRILL

Sassafras Saloon,
Los Angeles

Bartending at the
crowded Sassafras
Saloon has made Grill
the master of the four-
ingredient cocktail, like
her perfectly balanced
Nightcap (p. 168). "My
style of bartending is
keeping things simple.
Sometimes I work
with new and modern
techniques—mainly
barrel-aging—but I
try to stay as close to
home as possible," she
says. Her ever-evolving
cocktail list may riff
on past favorites, but
it rarely repeats itself.
She's also a Certified
Cicerone. *1233 N. Vine St.;*
sassafrashollywood.com.

ALBA HUERTA

Julep, Houston

Huerta, the first lady
of Houston mixology,
juggles shifts at cocktail
destination Anvil Bar
& Refuge, the mezcal-
centric spot The Pastry
War and now her own
bar, the Southern-
cocktail-focused Julep.
Her technically complex,
visually stunning
drinks—like the Burnt-
Spice Julep (p. 154),
made with a flaming
spice ball—appeal to all
the senses and prove
that Huerta's not afraid,
as she says, "to wave
my nerd flag high."
1919 Washington Ave.;
julephouston.com.

GUI JAROSCHY
The Broken Shaker, Miami Beach

The tiki authority of Miami Beach, Jaroschy uses ultra-fresh tropical fruit juices to create fun drinks that reflect the new school of tiki: not too sweet, but balanced and bracing. Though he's passionate about well-made cocktails, he maintains an air of levity at the bar and in his drinks. He serves playful, shareable big-batch cocktails–Bitches' Brew arrives in a hollowed-out watermelon with straws–and clever, cheekily named twists on classics, like Mel's Gibson (p. 180). "No matter where you are on the scale of seriousness, we can make something for you," he says. *2727 Indian Creek Dr.; thefreehand.com.*

SARA JUSTICE
The Franklin Mortgage & Investment Co., Philadelphia

Justice's cocktails have a definite sense of place. Inspired by the foods she ate growing up, the Pennsylvania-born bartender combines genever and aquavit to create the malt-inflected Eyeball Kid (p. 106); its hints of caraway and anise evoke Pennsylvania Dutch cooking. "I love putting work into each cocktail component," she says. "It allows you to build drinks that are full of flavor without using a lot of ingredients." *112 S. 18th St.; thefranklinbar.com.*

CAITLIN LAMAN
Trick Dog, San Francisco

Speed, creativity and accuracy won Laman the title of Miss Speed Rack USA 2014 at the national competition for top female bartenders. At Trick Dog, the atmosphere may be laid-back, but Laman's drinks are impeccable. "I was trained by Alex Bachman, now of Yusho in Chicago, under strict rules of how cocktails should be made," Laman says. Still, in the relaxed environment of Trick Dog, she's known for lighthearted concoctions like the Burnside Fizz (p. 70), a mix of Old Tom gin, coffee soda and cinnamon, topped with an egg white foam to evoke a cappuccino. *3010 20th St.; trickdogbar.com.*

JUSTIN LAVENUE
De Rigueur, Austin

Lavenue's bartending career began at an Indian restaurant, where he became adept at using South Asian herbs and spices in craft cocktails. At his upcoming bar, De Rigueur, he will stay true to his penchant for unconventional flavors and provide a "heightened drinking experience." One of his favorite drinks to make is April Showers Sour (p. 79), combining gin, vanilla yogurt and honeysuckle powder. "The cocktails that I come up with are a little more complicated. It's kind of like my personality in a drink," he says. *307 W. Fifth St.*

CHRIS LOWDER
The NoMad Bar, New York City

Lowder is serious about his drinks, but he also enjoys a little showboating behind the bar. "I get teased a lot by our staff because I have what you could call 'functional flair': little spins and tosses," he says. The bitters expert and former Japanese and Chinese language translator marries his skill in science-driven drink-making with an extensive knowledge of the classics. One example: Idle Hands (p. 156), a Manhattan variation enhanced with salt. *1170 Broadway; thenomadhotel.com.*

JEREMY OERTEL
Donna, Brooklyn

When he creates drinks, Oertel often starts with a classic and then tweaks it with innovative additions: His roasted cocoa nib amaro infuses the Magic Eight Ball (p. 170) with delicious chocolaty aromas. "You just have to think of the best way to get the flavors you're looking for," he says. "It's exciting how you can make riffs on riffs on riffs on riffs." But his style is always grounded in traditional ingredient combinations: "When you start to get lost, you can go back to the classics and find yourself again." *27 Broadway; donnabklyn.com.*

COLIN O'NEILL

Oyster House,
Philadelphia

A sculptor-turned-bartender, O'Neill often gets inspired by a specific ingredient, extracting its most potent flavor through a syrup or infusion. In his rum-and-Cognac-based Sir Greendown Punch (p. 114), for example, he transforms a drink using the nuances of spice in a chai tea syrup. His methodical tendencies inspired the squirrel tattoo on his arm. O'Neill explains: "My behaviors are very squirrel-like—I prepare for my shift with meticulous forethought. I've even been known to stash extra bar mops in secret hiding spots." *1516 Sansom St.; oysterhousephilly.com.*

JASON PATZ

Williams & Graham,
Denver

Patz's career has taken him from macro to micro: At 21, he began bartending at Chinese restaurant mega-chain P.F. Chang's; now he mixes exceptional drinks at the acclaimed bar-hidden-behind-a-bookcase Williams & Graham. International travel inspires his cocktails, like the Matcha Highball (p. 128), a green tea–laced concoction he created after exploring Japan. He eschews showy tricks in favor of a friendly attitude. "The only trick every bartender should know is basic conversation," he says. *3160 Tejon St.; williamsandgraham.com.*

SHANNON PONCHE

Mayahuel,
New York City

Savory elements distinguish Ponche's Latin-inspired cocktails: She plays with pairings like crema de mezcal (a blend of mezcal and agave nectar) and fresh sage (as in Sage Advice, p. 98) or tequila and apple cider vinegar (Coy Roy, p. 94). In addition to herbs and spices, she loves juices, "especially from a lot of different things that you wouldn't typically see in cocktails." For her signature sangritas, for example, she combines fresh pineapple juice with peach puree, smoked salt, pink peppercorn, habanero pepper and almond syrup. *304 E. Sixth St.; mayahuelny.com.*

ALEX RENSHAW
Bordel, Chicago

Working as a barback helped Renshaw pay for his first passion: improv comedy classes. But when he started to skip comedy class to cover bar shifts, he realized that he'd found his true calling. He's obsessed with exploring tropical flavors in drinks like Just Cause (p. 112), "a crazy French 75 variation" made with the sugarcane spirit cachaça. He's firmly rooted in tradition, though: He put 25 classics on the menu when he bartended at Drumbar; at Bordel, he mixes up frothy Ramos gin fizzes and large batches of pisco punch. *1721 W. Division St.; bordelchicago.com.*

TINA ROSS
Harvard & Stone, Los Angeles

Ross approaches mixology from a chef's perspective, using ingredients inspired by Harvard & Stone's largely Thai neighborhood. Cayenne and ginger crop up in cocktails like Firesuite (p. 40). She also likes to work with fresh produce. "We have such amazing agriculture here," she says. "Everything is available right outside your door." At the R&D Bar within H&S, she and guest bartenders create new drinks, testing out recipes and experimenting with offbeat ingredients. *5221 Hollywood Blvd.; harvardandstone.com.*

JAY SCHROEDER
Frontera Grill, Chicago

Schroeder's love affair with tequila, mezcal and its more florally nuanced relative sotol began when he bartended at the Latin-inspired Double A, Mercadito's basement bar in Chicago. With access to the restaurant's pantry, Schroeder familiarized himself with ingredients like panela sugar, ancho powder and guajillo chiles, which he likes to infuse into syrups or liquors. His cocktails at Frontera are also unmistakably Mexican. "We think of chiles as simply hot and spicy, but now I look at their flavor complexity," he says. *445 N. Clark St.; rickbayless.com.*

TYLER STEVENS

Teardrop Cocktail
Lounge, Portland, OR

Barista-turned-
bartender Stevens makes
edgy cocktails like Lady
Marmalade (p. 60), a
vodka drink mixed with
absinthe and tart verjus,
"to get people out of
their safe zone." He has
a particular fascination
with distinctly
Oregonian products,
like the Hood River pear
brandy in Crimson and
Clover (p. 59). His bar has
become an after-work
stop for local bartenders,
who like the staff's
nightly rendition of
Aaron Neville and Linda
Ronstadt's "Don't Know
Much." "It's our last-call
song," says Stevens,
"when we're taking off
the ties, starting to cut
loose." *1015 NW Everett
St.; teardroplounge.com.*

PAMELA WIZNITZER

Seamstress,
New York City

An ordinary night at
Seamstress might find
Wiznitzer dancing
behind the bar ("I tend to
do the Running Man, but
I can do the Robot, too")
or telling corny jokes
("Inevitably, really bad
ones always come out of
my mouth"). She does
all of this while speedily
turning out fantastic
cocktails like the frothy
whiskey-and-banana-
liqueur-based Fortitude
(p. 144) and the pear-
and-absinthe-inflected
11th Round (p. 134). "My
goal is to internalize
what you want and
transform it into
something delicious in
the glass in front of you,"
she says. *339 E. 75th St.;
seamstressny.com.*

SEAN WOODS

Deadhorse Hill,
Worcester,
Massachusetts

Time spent cooking in
elite kitchens like Craigie
on Main in Cambridge
means that Woods has
an appreciation for
savory cocktails. He's
also a master problem
solver when it comes to
utilizing an abundance
of unexpected
ingredients–for example,
transforming extra
fresh hops from a
local farmer into a
delicious syrup for the
whiskey-based Bells of St.
Clement's (p. 186). "In the
restaurant, there's always
an ingredient excess,"
he explains. "Once the
kitchen is done with it,
it comes to me. I always
take it." *38 Franklin St.;
deadhorsehill.com.*

HOMEMADE MIXERS

SIMPLE SYRUP

Makes about 12 ounces

In a small saucepan, combine 8 ounces water and 1 cup sugar and bring to a boil. Simmer over moderate heat, stirring frequently, until the sugar dissolves, about 3 minutes. Remove from the heat and let cool. Transfer the syrup to a bottle or tightly covered jar and refrigerate for up to 1 month.

RICH SIMPLE SYRUP

Makes about 8 ounces

In a small saucepan, combine 4 ounces water and 1 cup Demerara or other raw sugar and bring to a boil. Simmer over moderate heat, stirring, until the sugar dissolves, about 3 minutes. Remove from the heat and let cool.

Transfer the syrup to a bottle or tightly covered jar and refrigerate for up to 1 month.

EASIEST SIMPLE SYRUP

Makes about 12 ounces

In a bottle or jar with a tight-fitting lid, combine 8 ounces hot water with 1 cup superfine sugar and shake until the sugar dissolves. Let the syrup cool, then refrigerate for up to 1 month.

HOMEMADE GRENADINE

Makes about 12 ounces

In a bottle or jar with a tight-fitting lid, shake 8 ounces unsweetened pomegranate juice with 1 cup sugar until the sugar dissolves. If desired, add $1/8$ teaspoon orange flower water. Refrigerate for up to 2 weeks.

HONEY SYRUP

Makes about 6 ounces

In a microwavable bottle or jar, heat 4 ounces honey in a microwave for about 30 seconds at high power. Add 2 ounces warm water, cover tightly and shake until the honey dissolves. (Alternatively, in a small saucepan, stir 4 ounces honey and 2 ounces water over moderate heat until the honey dissolves.) Let cool, then refrigerate for up to 1 month.

DEEP PURPLE, REPRISE, P. 48

APERITIFS

VODKA
GIN
TEQUILA
RUM
WHISKEY
BRANDY
NIGHTCAPS
BIG BATCH
MOCKTAILS

FIRESUITE

Makes **1**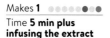

Time **5 min plus infusing the extract**

Mixologist Tina Ross of Harvard & Stone in Los Angeles created this fiery Pimm's Cup variation with St. George Dry Rye Gin. "I love this spirit," Ross says. "Compared to other gins, it's so strange—really tangy, and kind of straight-up evergreen in your face."

1½ oz. Pimm's No. 1 (gin-based aperitif)
1 oz. St. George Dry Rye Gin
¾ oz. Ginger Syrup (p. 82)
¾ oz. fresh lime juice
3 drops of Cayenne Extract (below)
   Ice
¾ oz. chilled club soda
1 cucumber spear and 1 mint sprig, for garnish

In a cocktail shaker, combine the Pimm's, gin, Ginger Syrup, lime juice and Cayenne Extract. Fill the shaker with ice and shake well. Strain into a chilled, ice-filled collins glass and stir in the club soda. Garnish with the cucumber spear and mint sprig. —*Tina Ross*

CAYENNE EXTRACT

In a liquid measuring cup, stir 2 oz. water with 1½ Tbsp. cayenne pepper and let stand for about 30 minutes. Strain the extract through cheesecloth or a coffee filter into a small jar and store at room temperature for up to 3 weeks. Makes about 2 oz. —*TR*

● STRONG ● SWEET ● TART ● BITTER ● FRUITY ● HERBAL ● SMOKY ● SPICY

KINGDOM OF RUST

Makes **1** ●●●●○●○○○○

"Amaro Montenegro is sweet, bitter and bright," says L.A. mixologist Tina Ross. *"This one ingredient basically has all the different flavors that you try to achieve in a cocktail."* She adds single-malt whiskey for a subtle hit of smoke.

1½ oz. **Amaro Montenegro**
¾ oz. **orgeat (almond-flavored syrup)**
¾ oz. **fresh lime juice**
  Ice
½ oz. **single-malt whiskey**
1 **lime twist, for garnish**

In a mixing glass, combine the amaro, orgeat and lime juice. Fill the glass with ice and stir for 10 seconds. Strain into a chilled, ice-filled rocks glass and float the whiskey on top, slowly pouring it over the back of a bar spoon near the drink's surface. Pinch the lime twist over the drink and add to the glass. —*Tina Ross*

LATE HARVEST

Makes **1** ●●○○●○●○○○

When Karen Fu was bartending at Momofuku Ssäm Bar and NoMad in New York City, she learned a lot about wines from the sommeliers and became a fan of Riesling. For this muddled-grape cocktail, she evokes the flavors of a late-harvest Riesling by combining dry Riesling with elderflower liqueur.

4 **green grapes**
½ oz. **Simple Syrup (p. 37)**
1½ oz. **chilled dry Riesling**
½ oz. **St-Germain elderflower liqueur**
½ oz. **fresh lemon juice**
3 **ice cubes**
1 oz. **chilled brut Champagne or other dry sparkling wine**

In a cocktail shaker, muddle the grapes with the Simple Syrup. Add the Riesling, St-Germain, lemon juice and ice. Shake well and fine-strain (p. 27) into a chilled flute. Top with the Champagne. —*Karen Fu*

FRESH AIR

Makes **1** ●●●●●●●●●

A shandy meets a gin sour in this fragrant aperitif from L.A. bartender Tina Ross. For the white ale stirred in at the end, she recommends one with orange and coriander flavors such as Avery White Rascal or Blanche de Bruxelles.

2	**half-moon orange slices**
6	**thyme sprigs**
1	**oz. London dry gin**
¾	**oz. French blanc vermouth, such as Dolin**
¾	**oz. fresh lemon juice**
½	**oz. Simple Syrup (p. 37)**
	Ice
1	**oz. chilled Belgian-style white ale**

In a cocktail shaker, muddle the orange slices with 5 of the thyme sprigs. Add the gin, vermouth, lemon juice and Simple Syrup. Fill the shaker with ice, shake well and fine-strain (p. 27) into a chilled white wine glass half-filled with ice. Stir in the ale and garnish with the remaining thyme sprig. —*Tina Ross*

AFTERNOON PILOT

Makes **1** ●●●●●●●●●

Karen Fu, bartender at The Happiest Hour in New York City, created this homage to the Paper Plane— a modern classic that's equal parts bourbon, lemon juice, Aperol and Amaro Nonino. Fu swaps in strawberries and sweet vermouth for the bourbon.

1½	**strawberries**
¾	**oz. Aperol**
¾	**oz. Amaro Nonino**
¾	**oz. fresh lemon juice**
½	**oz. Carpano Antica Formula or other sweet vermouth**
	Ice

In a cocktail shaker, muddle the whole strawberry. Add the Aperol, amaro, lemon juice and vermouth. Fill the shaker with ice and shake well. Fine-strain (p. 27) into a chilled coupe and garnish with the half strawberry. —*Karen Fu*

THE COUNTY FAIR FIX

Makes **1**

Manhattan bartender Karen Fu came up with this sherry–apple cider aperitif after a binge on cider doughnuts at a New Jersey apple farm. "The tart Granny Smith apple in this drink lightens the sweetness," says Fu.

Three ¼-inch-thick wedges of **Granny Smith apple**
¾ tsp. **Honey Syrup (p. 37)**
1 oz. **Lillet blanc**
1 oz. **amontillado sherry, preferably Lustau**
½ oz. **chilled apple cider**
2 dashes of **The Bitter Truth aromatic bitters**
3 **ice cubes**

In a cocktail shaker, muddle the apple wedges with the Honey Syrup. Add the Lillet, sherry, apple cider, bitters and ice cubes. Shake briefly and strain into a chilled coupe. —*Karen Fu*

LAST BROADCAST

Makes **1**

L.A. mixologist Tina Ross has been tinkering with this drink for years. She makes the rendition here with the nicely bitter aperitif Cynar. "Each time I make a new version, people say, 'Don't change it!'–but I do and they love it."

2 medium **strawberries, sliced,** plus 1 slice for garnish
1½ oz. **tawny port**
¾ oz. **pineapple gum syrup (see Note)**
½ oz. **Cynar (bitter artichoke aperitif)**
½ oz. **fresh lemon juice**
Ice
¾ oz. **chilled dry sparkling wine**
3 dashes of **absinthe**

In a cocktail shaker, muddle the 2 strawberries. Add the port, gum syrup, Cynar and lemon juice. Fill the shaker with ice, shake well and fine-strain (p. 27) into a large chilled coupe. Top with the sparkling wine and absinthe and garnish with the strawberry slice. —*Tina Ross*

Note Pineapple gum syrup, thickened pineapple-flavored simple syrup, is available from *smallhandfoods.com*.

● STRONG ● SWEET ● TART ● BITTER ● FRUITY ● HERBAL ● SMOKY ● SPICY

LAST BROADCAST

DEEP PURPLE, REPRISE

Makes **1** ●●●●●●●●

New York City mixologist Karen Fu adores the "inky purpleness" of this aperitif, which gets its color from Lillet rouge. She also loves shiso; here she muddles the Japanese herb with grapes. "It has a beautiful leaf design and a slight fennel flavor that can be a pleasant surprise," she says.

📷 p. 38

For a mocktail variation, see p. 198.

6	Concord grapes
2	shiso leaves
½	oz. Simple Syrup (p. 37)
1¾	oz. tawny port
1½	oz. Lillet rouge
¾	oz. French blanc vermouth, such as Dolin
3	ice cubes, plus crushed ice (p. 27) for serving
2	oz. chilled club soda

In a cocktail shaker, muddle the grapes and 1 shiso leaf with the Simple Syrup. Add the port, Lillet, vermouth and ice cubes. Shake well and fine-strain (p. 27) into a chilled, crushed-ice-filled rocks glass. Top with the club soda and garnish with the remaining shiso leaf. —*Karen Fu*

CLASSIC

AMERICANO

Makes **1** ●●●●●●●●●

This drink was a favorite of American expats in Italy during Prohibition. Before then it was known as the Milano-Torino, for the cities where its two main ingredients were first made: Milan (Campari) and Turin (sweet vermouth).

1½	oz. Campari
1½	oz. sweet vermouth
3	oz. chilled club soda
	Ice
1	orange wheel, for garnish

Pour the Campari, vermouth and club soda into a chilled rocks glass. Fill the glass with ice, stir briefly and garnish with the orange wheel.

● STRONG ● SWEET ● TART ● BITTER ● FRUITY ● HERBAL ● SMOKY ● SPICY

CLASSIC

MICHELADA

Makes 1

"You can make micheladas with tomato or Clamato juice–depending on personal preference," says Damian Windsor, bartender at the Roger Room in L.A. He makes his version of the Mexican classic with tomato juice.

- 2 oz. chilled tomato juice
- 1 oz. fresh lime juice
- ¾ oz. Simple Syrup (p. 37)
- 4 dashes of Maggi seasoning or Worcestershire sauce
- 2 dashes of hot sauce
- 2 pinches of sea salt
  Ice
- 12 oz. chilled lager, preferably Mexican

In a chilled pint glass, combine the tomato juice, lime juice, Simple Syrup, Maggi seasoning, hot sauce and 1 pinch of sea salt. Fill the glass three-quarters full with ice and stir well. Stir in enough lager to fill the glass and garnish with another pinch of salt. As you finish the drink, continue to pour in more lager.

CLASSIC

PIMM'S CUP

Makes 1

Wimbledon spectators drink ten to fifteen thousand Pimm's Cups every day while at the famous English tennis tournament. Americans often make the low-alcohol cocktail with Sprite or 7-Up, but the British use bitter lemon soda.

- 2 oz. Pimm's No. 1 (gin-based aperitif)
- 4 oz. chilled bitter lemon soda (see Note)
  Ice
- 1 each lemon wedge, apple slice and cucumber spear, for garnish

Pour the Pimm's and lemon soda into a chilled collins glass. Fill the glass with ice and stir briefly. Garnish with the lemon wedge, apple slice and cucumber spear.

Note Schweppes and Fever-Tree make high-quality, widely available bitter lemon sodas.

CHAMPAGNE COCKTAIL

Makes **1** ●●●●●●●●

According to master mixologist Dale DeGroff, this is one of the few original cocktails in the first (1862) edition of the seminal How to Mix Drinks *by Jerry Thomas. The recipe has remained unchanged for 150 years.*

5 oz. chilled Champagne
2 dashes of Angostura bitters
1 sugar cube
1 spiral-cut lemon twist (p. 26), for garnish

Pour the Champagne into a chilled flute. Sprinkle the bitters on the sugar cube and add to the flute. Garnish with the lemon twist.

APEROL SPRITZ

Makes **1** ●●●●●●●●

The origin of this drink can be traced back to Italy in the 1800s, when the country was occupied by Austria. Legend has it that the beer-loving Hapsburg soldiers found the local wine too strong, so they diluted it with sparkling water.

3 oz. chilled Prosecco
3 oz. chilled club soda
1½ oz. Aperol
Ice
1 orange slice, for garnish

In a large chilled wineglass, combine the Prosecco, club soda and Aperol. Fill the glass with ice, stir briefly, then garnish with the orange slice.

● STRONG ● SWEET ● TART ● BITTER ● FRUITY ● HERBAL ● SMOKY ● SPICY

CHAMPAGNE
COCKTAIL

OF MOUNTAINS AND VALLEYS, P. 59

VODKA

APERITIFS
GIN
TEQUILA
RUM
WHISKEY
BRANDY
NIGHTCAPS
BIG BATCH
MOCKTAILS

SECONDHAND NEWS

Makes **1** ●●●●●●●●●

Tyler Stevens, bar manager at Teardrop Cocktail Lounge in Portland, Oregon, adds heft to this vodka drink with sherry and Génépy des Alpes, an herbal liqueur that has recently become available in the US. Made from the same rare Alpine plant as Chartreuse, Génépy liqueur is a very popular item at French ski resorts.

1 oz. vodka
¾ oz. fino sherry
¾ oz. orgeat (almond-flavored syrup)
½ oz. Dolin Génépy des Alpes
  or yellow Chartreuse
½ oz. fresh lemon juice
¼ oz. Rich Simple Syrup (p. 37)
  Ice cubes, plus crushed ice (p. 27) for serving
3 red apple slices, fanned out and skewered
  on a pick, and 1 thyme sprig, for garnish

In a cocktail shaker, combine the vodka, sherry, orgeat, Génépy, lemon juice and Rich Simple Syrup. Fill the shaker with ice cubes and shake briefly. Strain into a chilled, crushed-ice-filled highball glass and garnish with the skewered apples and thyme sprig. —*Tyler Stevens*

THE OSTERIA OUTING

Makes **1** ●●●●●●●●●

Jacyara de Oliveira envisioned a casual Italian restaurant as the ideal setting for her pleasantly powerful drink.

2 oz. vodka
1 oz. Moscatel or other sweet sherry
¾ oz. Amaro Nonino
  Dash of Angostura bitters
  Ice
1 grapefruit twist, for garnish

In a mixing glass, combine the vodka, sherry, amaro and bitters. Fill the glass with ice, stir well and strain into a chilled coupe. Pinch the twist over the drink and add to the coupe.
—*Jacyara de Oliveira*

● STRONG ● SWEET ● TART ● BITTER ● FRUITY ● HERBAL ● SMOKY ● SPICY

THE THISTLE IN THE KISS

Makes **1** ●●○○○●○○

Time **5 min plus steeping the syrup**

During a bartending gig at a restaurant, Chicago mixologist Jacyara de Oliveira took fennel scraps from the kitchen to infuse a simple syrup. Now, as head bartender at Sportsman's Club, she uses fennel syrup to add a mild anise flavor to drinks. The syrup would also be fantastic in lemonade and hot and iced teas.

For a mocktail variation, see p. 200.

1½ oz. vodka
¾ oz. fresh lime juice
¾ oz. Fennel Syrup (below)
½ oz. Suze (French gentian aperitif)
    Ice
    1 or 2 basil leaves, smacked (p. 27), for garnish

In a cocktail shaker, combine the vodka, lime juice, Fennel Syrup and Suze. Fill the shaker with ice and shake well. Strain into a chilled, ice-filled rocks glass and garnish with the smacked basil.
—*Jacyara de Oliveira*

FENNEL SYRUP

In a saucepan, boil 4 oz. water. Remove from the heat, add ½ cup cubed fennel (½-inch pieces cut from ½ small bulb) and let steep for 6 minutes. Remove and discard the fennel. Add ½ cup sugar to the saucepan and bring to a boil, stirring until dissolved. Remove from the heat, let cool and transfer the syrup to a jar. Refrigerate for up to 2 weeks. Makes about 6 oz. —*Chris Lowder*

●STRONG ●SWEET ○TART ●BITTER ●FRUITY ●HERBAL ●SMOKY ●SPICY

THE BIRDS AND THE BLOSSOMS

Makes **1**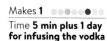

Time **5 min plus 1 day for infusing the vodka**

For many people, flavored vodkas are tacky. Not for Jacyara de Oliveira, who uses house-made seasonal ones at Sportsman's Club in Chicago. Here, she spikes vodka with fresh lemon verbena leaves (available at farmers' markets and nurseries) to add a delicate floral-citrus flavor.

For a mocktail variation, see p. 196.

For a mocktail variation, see p. 196.

1½ oz. Lemon Verbena Vodka (below)
1½ oz. white vermouth, such as Dolin blanc
¾ oz. fresh lemon juice
½ oz. Honey Syrup (p. 37)
　　Ice
1½ oz. chilled club soda
1 lemon balm sprig, for garnish (optional)
¼ oz. absinthe, in an atomizer

In a chilled collins glass, combine the Lemon Verbena Vodka, vermouth, lemon juice and Honey Syrup. Fill the glass with ice and stir well. Stir in the club soda and garnish with the lemon balm sprig. Spritz the drink with the absinthe.
—*Jacyara de Oliveira*

LEMON VERBENA VODKA

In a jar, combine 8 oz. vodka with 1 lightly packed cup fresh lemon verbena and shake vigorously; let stand for 24 hours. Pour the infused vodka through a fine-mesh strainer and refrigerate for up to 3 weeks. Makes about 8 oz. —*JDO*

● STRONG ● SWEET ○ TART ● BITTER ● FRUITY ● HERBAL ● SMOKY ● SPICY

CRIMSON AND CLOVER

Makes 1

Tyler Stevens serves this autumn sour at Teardrop Cocktail Lounge in Portland, Oregon. He makes it with local Dystopia vodka and Clear Creek pear brandy, which is distilled from pears grown in nearby Hood River.

1 oz. vodka
1 oz. pear brandy, preferably Clear Creek
¾ oz. Amaro CioCiaro
¾ oz. fresh grapefruit juice
½ oz. Honey Syrup (p. 37)
¼ oz. fresh lemon juice
   Ice, plus 1 large cube for serving
1 sage leaf, smacked (p. 27), for garnish

In a cocktail shaker, combine the vodka, pear brandy, amaro, grapefruit juice, Honey Syrup and lemon juice. Fill the shaker with ice and shake well. Strain into a chilled rocks glass over the large ice cube and garnish with the smacked sage leaf. —*Tyler Stevens*

OF MOUNTAINS AND VALLEYS

Makes 1

"Between spirits, liqueurs, citrus and syrup, a cocktail can get really disjointed," says Jacyara de Oliveira. For a more cohesive drink, she uses neutral vodka to bring all the elements together.

📷 p. 52

1½ oz. potato vodka, such as Karlsson's Gold
¾ oz. Velvet Falernum (clove-spiced liqueur)
¾ oz. fresh lemon juice
½ oz. Highland Scotch, such as Glenmorangie
¼ oz. Honey Syrup (p. 37)
   Dash of lavender bitters
   Ice
1 fresh violet, for garnish (optional)

In a cocktail shaker, combine the vodka, Velvet Falernum, lemon juice, Scotch, Honey Syrup and bitters. Fill the shaker with ice and shake well. Strain into a chilled coupe and garnish with the violet. —*Jacyara de Oliveira*

LADY MARMALADE

Makes **1** ●●○○○○○○○○

"I created Lady Marmalade to get people out of their safe zone," says Tyler Stevens, bar manager at Teardrop Cocktail Lounge in Portland, Oregon. "The sweet ingredients like grenadine and ginger liqueur are balanced by the absinthe rinse to create a crisp, aromatic drink."

For a mocktail variation, see p. 198.

¼ oz. absinthe
1 oz. vodka
1 oz. French blanc vermouth, such as Dolin
½ oz. ginger liqueur, preferably Domaine de Canton
¼ oz. chilled verjus (see Note)
1 tsp. grenadine, preferably homemade (p. 37)
   Ice

Rinse a chilled coupe with the absinthe; pour out the excess. In a mixing glass, combine the vodka, vermouth, ginger liqueur, verjus and grenadine. Fill the glass with ice and stir well. Strain into the prepared coupe. —*Tyler Stevens*

Note Verjus, the tart juice pressed from unripe grapes, is available at specialty food stores.

A MORE PERFECT UNION

Makes **1** ●○○○○●○○○

Tyler Stevens made this cocktail for a guest who told him, "I'm a vodka martini drinker, but I feel bad for ordering something so plain." Stevens says this variation on a Vesper "has the clean and streamlined style that guest was looking for."

1¼ oz. Lillet blanc
¾ oz. vodka, preferably Belvedere
¼ oz. apricot liqueur
   Ice
1 grapefruit twist, for garnish

In a mixing glass, combine the Lillet, vodka and apricot liqueur. Fill the glass with ice, stir well and strain into a chilled coupe. Pinch the grapefruit twist over the drink and add to the coupe. —*Tyler Stevens*

●STRONG ●SWEET ●TART ●BITTER ●FRUITY ●HERBAL ●SMOKY ●SPICY

CLASSIC

BLOODY MARY

Makes **1** ⬤⬤⬤⬤⬤⬤⬤⬤⬤●

These days Bloody Marys are garnished with anything from olives and pickles to lobster claws and bacon cheeseburgers. Craig Schoettler, mixologist for Aria Resort and Casino in Las Vegas, keeps it classic with celery and lemon.

8	oz. chilled tomato juice
1½	oz. vodka
¼	oz. fresh lemon juice
½	tsp. Worcestershire sauce, plus more to taste
½	tsp. Tabasco, plus more to taste
	Ice
	Salt and freshly ground pepper
1	celery rib and 1 lemon wedge, for garnish

In a chilled collins glass, combine the tomato juice, vodka, lemon juice, Worcestershire sauce and Tabasco. Fill the glass with ice and stir well. Season the drink with salt and pepper and garnish with the celery rib and lemon wedge.

CLASSIC

COSMOPOLITAN

Makes **1** ⬤⬤○○○⬤○○○

After the TV show Sex and the City popularized the cosmopolitan, it became so trendy that bartenders began to hate mixing it. Today, the pink drink is making a comeback. It's even inspired the hashtag #cosbros on social media for men who love drinking it.

2½	oz. lemon vodka
1	oz. triple sec
1	oz. chilled cranberry juice
1½	tsp. fresh lime juice
	Ice
1	lemon twist, for garnish

In a cocktail shaker, combine the vodka, triple sec, cranberry juice and lime juice. Fill the shaker with ice, shake well and strain into a chilled martini glass. Pinch the lemon twist over the drink and add to the glass.

MOSCOW MULE

Makes **1** ●●○○○○○○●

Traditionally served in a frosty copper mug, the Moscow Mule helped vodka become popular in the US in the 1940s. Previously, one American cocktail book had described vodka as "Russian for 'horrendous.'"

- ½ **lime, plus 1 lime wheel for garnish**
- 2 **oz. vodka**
  Ice
- 4 **oz. chilled ginger beer**

Squeeze ½ oz. lime juice into a chilled copper mug or collins glass and drop in the spent lime shell. Add the vodka, fill the mug with ice and stir well. Stir in the ginger beer and garnish with the lime wheel.

KAMIKAZE

Makes **1 or 2**
●○○○○○○○○

Often associated with high-octane shots and happy-hour specials, the kamikaze has a history that can be traced back to a bar on the American naval base in Yokosuka, Japan, during the late 1940s or early '50s. Today, famed mixologist Hidetsugo Ueno of Bar High Five in Tokyo makes a less sweet version, using a higher ratio of lime juice to triple sec.

- 1½ **oz. vodka**
- ½ **oz. fresh lime juice**
- 2 **tsp. Cointreau or other triple sec**
  Ice

In a cocktail shaker, combine the vodka, lime juice and Cointreau. Fill the shaker with ice and shake well. Strain into a chilled, ice-filled rocks glass or 2 shot glasses.

● STRONG ● SWEET ○ TART ● BITTER ● FRUITY ● HERBAL ● SMOKY ● SPICY

MARTINI (LEFT), P. 86
DEAN STREET, P. 69

APERITIFS
VODKA

GIN

TEQUILA
RUM
WHISKEY
BRANDY
NIGHTCAPS
BIG BATCH
MOCKTAILS

NOUVEAU WESTERN

Makes **1** ●●○○○○○○○○

Austin mixologist Justin Lavenue muddles a cardamom pod into this fresh, floral club soda–topped drink. It's a nod to his first bartending job, at an Indian restaurant in Boulder, where he often incorporated spices into cocktails.

1	**cardamom pod**
1¼	**oz. Simple Syrup (p. 37)**
1½	**oz. New Western gin, such as Aviation**
1½	**oz. nigori sake**
1	**oz. Cocchi Americano (fortified, slightly bitter aperitif wine)**
4	**dashes of orange bitters**
	Ice
2	**oz. chilled club soda**
1	**lime twist and 1 thyme sprig, for garnish**

In a chilled collins glass, muddle the cardamom with the Simple Syrup. Add the gin, sake, Cocchi and bitters. Fill the glass with ice and stir well. Discard the cardamom, then stir in the club soda. Pinch the lime twist over the drink, drop it in and garnish with the thyme sprig. —*Justin Lavenue*

LITTLE MONTANA

Makes **1** ●○○○○○○○○○

At Cane & Table in New Orleans, Nick Detrich loves using Spanish ingredients like pacharán. The anise-flavored digestif was a favorite of Spanish royalty in the 15th century and is now gaining recognition among US mixologists.

1	**oz. London dry gin, such as Fords**
1	**oz. pacharán (liqueur made from sloe berries, smaller, tart cousins of damson plums)**
1	**oz. French dry vermouth, such as Dolin**
2	**dashes of orange bitters**
	Ice
1	**lemon twist, for garnish**

In a mixing glass, combine the gin, pacharán, vermouth and bitters. Fill the glass with ice, stir well and strain into a chilled coupe. Pinch the lemon twist over the drink and add to the coupe. —*Nick Detrich*

● STRONG ● SWEET ◐ TART ● BITTER ● FRUITY ● HERBAL ● SMOKY ● SPICY

3'S AWAY

Makes **1** ●●●●●●●●●●

When Chad Arnholt tended bar at Trick Dog in San Francisco, he made this drink for a customer with a stomach ache. He wanted something minty and citrusy but without any citrus juice.

1½ oz. London dry gin, preferably Bombay
¾ oz. Calvados
¾ oz. Cocchi Americano (fortified, slightly bitter aperitif wine)
5 mint leaves
Ice
1 grapefruit twist

In a mixing glass, combine the gin, Calvados, Cocchi Americano and mint. Fill the glass with ice, stir well and strain into a chilled coupe. Pinch the grapefruit twist over the drink and discard. —*Chad Arnholt*

DEAN STREET

Makes **1** ●●●●●●●●●

Named after the street in Brooklyn where she first tried sherry, Dean Street is Caitlin Laman's riff on a sherry cobbler. "Sherry is my current go-to drink and mixer," says Laman, a bartender at Trick Dog in San Francisco.

📷 p. 66

2 strawberries, 2 blueberries and 2 blackberries
1 oz. aquavit (caraway-flavored spirit)
1 oz. amontillado sherry
¾ oz. orgeat (almond-flavored syrup), preferably Small Hand Foods (smallhandfoods.com)
¾ oz. fresh lemon juice
Crushed ice (p. 27)

In a cocktail shaker, muddle 1 strawberry, 1 blueberry and 1 blackberry. Add the aquavit, sherry, orgeat and lemon juice. Fill the shaker with crushed ice, shake briefly and pour into a chilled julep cup or rocks glass. Top with more crushed ice. Skewer the remaining berries on a pick and garnish the drink. —*Caitlin Laman*

BURNSIDE FIZZ

Makes **1** ●●○○○○○○○

Time **5 min plus steeping the syrup**

With coffee soda, cinnamon and a frothy head of egg white, Burnside Fizz simulates the appearance of a cappuccino. According to the cocktail's creator, Caitlin Laman, "It's fun and light and meant to be drunk quickly. It's also really good when you make it with mezcal."

2   oz. Old Tom gin
¾   oz. fresh lemon juice
½   oz. Cinnamon Syrup (below)
1   large egg white
    Ice
3   oz. chilled coffee soda
1   lemon twist

In a cocktail shaker, combine the gin, lemon juice, Cinnamon Syrup and egg white. Shake vigorously. Fill the shaker with ice and shake again. Strain into a chilled fizz or highball glass and stir in the coffee soda. Pinch the lemon twist over the drink and discard. —*Caitlin Laman*

CINNAMON SYRUP
In a small saucepan, combine 1 cup sugar, 4 oz. water and three 2-inch cinnamon sticks broken into large pieces. Cook over moderately low heat, stirring frequently, until the sugar dissolves, about 5 minutes. Remove from the heat and let cool. Discard the cinnamon. Transfer the syrup to a jar and refrigerate for up to 3 weeks. Makes about 8 oz. —*CL*

● STRONG ● SWEET ○ TART ● BITTER ● FRUITY ● HERBAL ● SMOKY ● SPICY

BURNSIDE FIZZ

POUR MA GUEULE (FOR MY MOUTH)

Makes **1** ●●●●●●●●●

Justin Lavenue modeled this drink after Sancerre. To get the wine's characteristic flintiness, he seasons the serving glass with smoke captured from ignited dried lemon peel and cinnamon-like cassia bark. The name of the drink, Pour Ma Gueule, is a French term used by vintners for wine that is so good that it should not be bottled for public consumption but saved for family and friends.

1½ oz. London dry gin
1½ oz. French dry vermouth, such as Dolin
1½ oz. cold water
¼ oz. maraschino liqueur
¼ oz. chilled verjus (see Note)
3 dashes of orange bitters
2 dashes of absinthe verte
Ice
1 Tbsp. cassia chips (see Note)
1 tsp. minced dried lemon peel
1 lemon twist and 1 grapefruit twist

1. In a mixing glass, combine the gin, vermouth, water, maraschino liqueur, verjus, bitters and absinthe. Fill the glass with ice and stir well.

2. In a ramekin, combine the cassia chips and dried lemon peel. Carefully light them with a long-handled match. The spices will start to smoke. Invert a white wine glass over the ramekin and allow the smoke to season the inside of the glass for 20 to 30 seconds.

3. Strain the drink into the prepared wineglass. Pinch the lemon and then the grapefruit twists over the drink and discard them. —*Justin Lavenue*

Note Verjus, the tart juice pressed from unripe grapes, is available at specialty food stores. Cassia chips, cinnamon-flavored bark from Asia, are available from *kalustyans.com*.

● STRONG ● SWEET ○ TART ● BITTER ● FRUITY ● HERBAL ● SMOKY ● SPICY

THE DANISH FLY

Makes **1** ●●●●●●●●

New Orleans bartender Nick Detrich concocted this drink when he and Neal Bodenheimer, his business partner at Cane & Table, had a contest to pair banana and caraway. ("Finding out that banana molecules are almost identical to those in caraway prompted this flavor exploration," Detrich says.) When Bodenheimer tasted Detrich's Danish Fly, made with the caraway-flavored spirit aquavit, he immediately conceded.

1 oz. aquavit, preferably Krogstad
1 oz. banana liqueur, preferably Giffard Banane du Brésil
1 oz. fresh lemon juice
½ oz. grenadine, preferably homemade (p. 37)
  Ice cubes, plus cracked ice (p. 27) or pebble ice (slightly larger and more rounded than crushed ice) for serving
1 lemon twist, for garnish

In a cocktail shaker, combine the aquavit, banana liqueur, lemon juice and grenadine. Fill the shaker with ice cubes, shake well and fine-strain (p. 27) into a chilled pilsner filled with cracked or pebble ice. Pinch the lemon twist over the drink and add to the glass. —*Nick Detrich*

● STRONG ● SWEET ● TART ● BITTER ● FRUITY ● HERBAL ● SMOKY ● SPICY

THE DANISH FLY

TWO PALMS

Makes **1** ● ● ● ● ● ● ● ● ●

Coconut water is the breakout beverage of the decade, but people were actually mixing it into cocktails back in the 1800s. Nick Detrich of Cane & Table in New Orleans read about it in Jeff "Beachbum" Berry's Potions of the Caribbean: 500 Years of Tropical Drinks and the People Behind Them. *Detrich recalls, "The recipe went something like, 'Crack an egg, drop it in the coconut. Shake it up and add some gin.'"*

1   oz. London dry gin, such as Beefeater
½   oz. fresh lime juice
½   oz. Simple Syrup (p. 37)
1   large egg white
     Ice
1   oz. chilled coconut water
     Pinch of freshly grated nutmeg, for garnish

In a cocktail shaker, combine the gin, lime juice, Simple Syrup and egg white. Shake vigorously. Fill the shaker with ice and shake again. Fine-strain (p. 27) into a chilled coupe. Stir the coconut water into the cocktail and garnish with the grated nutmeg. —*Nick Detrich*

● STRONG ● SWEET ● TART ● BITTER ● FRUITY ● HERBAL ● SMOKY ● SPICY

DEVIL'S CAT

Makes **1** ●●●●●●●●

Time **5 min plus steeping the syrup**

Chad Arnholt of The Perennial in San Francisco had an epiphany when he added gin to the usual rum in a daiquiri. "It was like, 'Whoa! Gin and rum love each other!'" For this tiki-style drink, he suggests a fruit-forward gin like Tanqueray Malacca—"It's very tropical, like a pineapple bomb." His other revelation when making Devil's Cat: "When you combine funky rum flavors with amaro and a tiny bit of spiciness, it tastes a little like jerk chicken."

1 oz. Tanqueray Malacca gin or Old Tom gin

¾ oz. Raspberry Syrup (below)
or Small Hand Foods raspberry gum syrup
(smallhandfoods.com)

¾ oz. fresh lime juice

½ oz. Batavia-Arrack van Oosten
(spicy, citrusy, rum-like spirit)

½ oz. Amaro Lucano
Small pinch of cayenne pepper
Ice cubes, plus crushed ice (p. 27) for serving

1 mint sprig and 3 raspberries, for garnish

In a cocktail shaker, combine the gin, Raspberry Syrup, lime juice, Batavia-Arrack, amaro and cayenne pepper. Fill the shaker with ice cubes and shake well. Strain into a chilled, crushed-ice-filled tiki mug or tall glass. Garnish with the mint sprig and raspberries. —*Chad Arnholt*

RASPBERRY SYRUP

In a medium saucepan, combine 4 oz. water with ¾ cup superfine sugar and 1½ cups raspberries. Cook over low heat for 15 minutes, smashing the raspberries. Remove from the heat and let stand for 30 minutes. Strain the syrup into a jar, cover and refrigerate for up to 4 days. Makes about 8 oz.

● STRONG ● SWEET ● TART ● BITTER ● FRUITY ● HERBAL ● SMOKY ● SPICY

APRIL SHOWERS SOUR

Makes **1** ●●●●●●●●

Time **5 min plus infusing the orgeat**

To add texture and creaminess without the cream, Austin mixologist Justin Lavenue shakes a little bit of vanilla yogurt into this floral gin sour. "It has a tartness that can balance out a drink and make it light and refreshing," he says.

One 1-inch piece of fresh lemongrass (tender inner bulb)

¾ oz. Lavender Orgeat (below)

1½ oz. Old Tom gin

½ oz. fresh grapefruit juice

¼ oz. fresh lemon juice

1 Tbsp. honeysuckle powder (optional; see Note)

1 Tbsp. whole-milk vanilla yogurt

Ice

3 drops of Peychaud's bitters, for garnish

In a cocktail shaker, muddle the lemongrass with the Lavender Orgeat. Add the gin, grapefruit juice, lemon juice, honeysuckle powder and yogurt. Fill the shaker with ice and shake well. Strain into a chilled coupe and garnish with the bitters.
—*Justin Lavenue*

LAVENDER ORGEAT

In a liquid measuring cup, combine 1 oz. dried lavender with 4 oz. orgeat (almond-flavored syrup) and let stand for 30 minutes. Strain the infused orgeat into a jar and refrigerate for up to 3 weeks. Makes about 4 oz. —*JL*

Note Honeysuckle powder is available at apothecaries and from *amazon.com*.

THE PERFECT BLOOM

Makes **1**

The Perfect Bloom was inspired by the smell of spring flowers after a sun shower. Austin mixologist Justin Lavenue loves to make the cocktail with a super-floral gin like Leopold's, which is distilled with bergamot. Alternatively, he recommends Hendrick's gin, which is infused with rose and cucumber.

¼ oz. 12-year Japanese whisky, such as Hakushu, in an atomizer
2 oz. floral gin
½ oz. French blanc vermouth, such as Dolin
½ oz. Amaro Montenegro
¼ oz. chilled verjus (see Note on p. 72)
Ice
3 thin cucumber slices and fresh lavender sprigs (optional), for garnish

Mist a chilled coupe with 4 sprays of the whisky. In a mixing glass, combine the gin, vermouth, amaro and verjus. Fill the glass with ice and stir well. Strain into the prepared coupe and garnish with the fanned-out cucumber slices and the lavender sprigs. —*Justin Lavenue*

PORT TOWNSEND NO. 2

Makes **1**

Caitlin Laman came up with this Old Tom gin cocktail at Trick Dog in San Francisco when a customer requested a riff on a Martinez. In place of the classic's maraschino liqueur, she stirs in nutty crème de noyaux.

1½ oz. Old Tom gin, preferably Ransom
1½ oz. Cocchi Vermouth di Torino (slightly bitter red vermouth)
¾ tsp. crème de noyaux (almond-flavored liqueur)
Ice
1 lemon twist, for garnish

In a mixing glass, combine the gin, vermouth and crème de noyaux. Fill the glass with ice, stir well and strain into a small chilled coupe. Pinch the lemon twist over the drink and add to the coupe. —*Caitlin Laman*

● STRONG ● SWEET ● TART ● BITTER ● FRUITY ● HERBAL ● SMOKY ● SPICY

FIDDLESTICKS AND HORSEFEATHERS

Makes **1**

Time **5 min plus steeping the syrup**

According to San Francisco mixologist Chad Arnholt, people often think of gin as a light and lean spirit. But genever, the predecessor to gin, has a malty, hearty, whiskey-like quality that's terrific in this old-fashioned-style drink. "Cocktail historian Dave Wondrich makes a strong case that the old-fashioneds of the 1800s might very well have been made with a malty, gin-like spirit," Arnholt says.

- 2 oz. Bols barrel-aged genever
- ¼ oz. crème de cassis (black-currant liqueur)
- ¾ tsp. Luxardo maraschino liqueur
- ⅜ tsp. Ginger Syrup (below)
- 2 dashes of orange bitters
  Ice, plus 1 large cube for serving
- 1 orange twist

In a mixing glass, combine the genever, crème de cassis, maraschino liqueur, Ginger Syrup and bitters. Fill the glass with ice, stir well and strain into a chilled rocks glass over the large ice cube. Pinch the orange twist over the drink and discard. —*Chad Arnholt*

GINGER SYRUP

In a small saucepan, combine ½ cup sugar with 4 oz. water. Simmer over moderate heat, stirring, until the sugar dissolves. Add ⅓ cup (1½ oz.) minced fresh ginger and simmer over very low heat for 30 minutes, stirring occasionally. Let cool, then pour the syrup through a fine strainer into a jar. Refrigerate for up to 2 weeks. Makes about 5 oz.

● STRONG ● SWEET ○ TART ● BITTER ● FRUITY ● HERBAL ● SMOKY ● SPICY

LOGAN SQUARE

Makes **1** ●●●●●●●●

In this take on a Negroni, Caitlin Laman of San Francisco's Trick Dog swaps out the usual gin for aquavit. It lends an elegant licorice flavor to the bittersweet cocktail.

1½   oz. aged aquavit, preferably Linie
½   oz. Gran Classico Bitter
     (bittersweet herbal liqueur)
½   oz. Cocchi Vermouth di Torino
     (slightly bitter red vermouth)
½   oz. French dry vermouth, such as Dolin
     Ice, plus 1 large cube for serving
1   lemon twist, for garnish

In a mixing glass, combine the aquavit, Gran Classico and both vermouths. Fill the glass with ice and stir well. Strain into a chilled double rocks glass over the large ice cube. Pinch the lemon twist over the drink and add to the glass.
—*Caitlin Laman*

A LESSER KEY

Makes **1** ●●●●●●●●

"This is a sturdy cocktail that's good to start or end the evening with," says Nick Detrich of Cane & Table in New Orleans. In addition to orange cream citrate (a tart tincture reminiscent of orange cream soda), he recommends making it with Tempus Fugit crème de menthe, which is a little richer than other brands and makes for a lusher drink.

¾   oz. genever, preferably Bols
¾   oz. French blanc vermouth, such as Dolin
¾   oz. pisco
¼   oz. white crème de menthe
14   drops of Bittermens orange cream citrate
     Dash of Angostura bitters
     Ice

In a mixing glass, combine the genever, vermouth, pisco, crème de menthe, orange cream citrate and bitters. Fill the glass with ice and stir well. Strain into a chilled coupe. —*Nick Detrich*

● STRONG ● SWEET ◐ TART ◐ BITTER ◐ FRUITY ● HERBAL ● SMOKY ● SPICY

FRENCH 75

Makes **1**

Many believe this drink was devised by American soldiers in France during World War I who were hankering for a Tom Collins. They had gin and lemons but no soda, so they used what was at hand: Champagne. The result was named for the French-made 75-millimeter guns.

1 oz. gin
½ oz. fresh lemon juice
½ oz. Simple Syrup (p. 37)
  Ice
4 oz. chilled brut Champagne

In a cocktail shaker, combine the gin, lemon juice and Simple Syrup. Fill the shaker with ice and shake well. Strain into a chilled flute and top with the Champagne.

CORPSE REVIVER NO. 2

Makes **1**

According to Harry Craddock's seminal Savoy Cocktail Book of 1930, this tart cocktail should be consumed as a pick-me-up. "But four of these taken in swift succession will unrevive the corpse again," he warns.

¼ oz. absinthe
1 oz. gin
1 oz. Cointreau or other triple sec
1 oz. Lillet blanc
1 oz. fresh lemon juice
  Ice

Rinse a chilled martini glass with the absinthe; pour out the excess. In a cocktail shaker, combine the gin, Cointreau, Lillet and lemon juice. Fill the shaker with ice, shake well and strain into the prepared martini glass.

NEGRONI

Makes **1** ●●○●○○○○○

This cocktail probably got its name from Camillo Negroni, a Florentine aristocrat who liked to add a splash of gin to his Americano (sweet vermouth, Campari and soda).

1   oz. gin
1   oz. sweet vermouth
1   oz. Campari
    Ice
    1 or 2 orange wheels, for garnish

In a mixing glass, combine the gin, vermouth and Campari. Fill the glass with ice and stir well. Strain into a chilled martini glass or coupe and garnish with the orange wheels. Alternatively, strain into a chilled, ice-filled rocks glass and garnish.

MARTINI

Makes **1** ●○○○○●○○○

The original martini, allegedly invented in the US in the 1860s, was made with sweet vermouth. One of the first recipes for a dry martini, made with dry vermouth, appeared in Frank P. Newman's 1904 American Bar.

📷 p. 66

3   oz. gin
1   oz. dry vermouth
2   dashes of orange bitters
    Ice
1   **green olive or 1 lemon twist, for garnish**

In a mixing glass, combine the gin, vermouth and bitters. Fill the glass with ice and stir well. Strain into a chilled martini glass or coupe and garnish with the olive or lemon twist.

● STRONG ● SWEET ○ TART ● BITTER ● FRUITY ● HERBAL ● SMOKY ● SPICY

AVIATION

Makes **1** ●○○○○○○○○○

The original, 1916 Aviation included crème de violette, a violet-flavored liqueur that tinted the drink a pale sky blue (hence the cocktail's name, some say). Later, the liqueur became impossible to find in the US, and a version without it became the standard. Ironically, at least three new brands of the liqueur have launched within the last decade.

2	oz. gin
¾	oz. fresh lemon juice
⅜	oz. maraschino liqueur
⅜	oz. crème de violette (violet liqueur)
	Ice
1	sour cherry, preferably marasca, for garnish (optional)

In a cocktail shaker, combine the gin, lemon juice, maraschino liqueur and violet liqueur. Fill the shaker with ice and shake well. Strain into a chilled coupe and garnish with the cherry.

BRONX

Makes **1** ○○○○○○○○○○

The Bronx became a popular drink around 1910, possibly because it was one of the first to contain orange juice. In 1934, Burke's Complete Cocktail and Drinking Recipes ranked it as the third most famous cocktail in the world, after the martini and the Manhattan.

1½	oz. London dry gin
1	oz. fresh orange juice
½	oz. sweet vermouth
½	oz. dry vermouth
	Ice

In a cocktail shaker, combine the gin, orange juice and both vermouths. Fill the shaker with ice and shake well. Strain into a chilled coupe.

● STRONG ● SWEET ○ TART ● BITTER ● FRUITY ● HERBAL ● SMOKY ● SPICY

AVIATION

PALOMA, P. 102

TEQUILA

MAGNETIC POLE REVERSAL

Makes **1** ●●●●●●●●●

Time **5 min plus making the puree**

"*Sotol is my absolute favorite spirit in the world,*" says Jay Schroeder, bar manager at Chicago's Frontera Grill, about this mezcal relative made from an agave-like plant. To highlight sotol's "vegetal and superfunky" flavors, leave some of the cucumber peel in the drink's basil-cucumber puree, as Schroeder does at Frontera.

For a mocktail variation, see p. 203.

1½ oz. blanco sotol, preferably Ocho Cientos
1½ oz. Basil-Cucumber Puree (below)
¾ oz. fresh lime juice
¾ oz. Simple Syrup (p. 37)
¼ oz. Salers or Suze (bittersweet gentian aperitifs)
    Ice
1 small basil sprig, for garnish

In a cocktail shaker, combine the sotol, Basil-Cucumber Puree, lime juice, Simple Syrup and Salers. Fill the shaker with ice and shake well. Strain into a chilled, ice-filled rocks glass and garnish with the basil sprig. —*Jay Schroeder*

BASIL-CUCUMBER PUREE

In a small saucepan, lightly toast 1 tsp. coriander seeds over low heat until fragrant, about 3 minutes. Transfer to a blender. Add 1 large peeled and seeded English cucumber and ⅓ cup basil leaves; puree until as smooth as possible. Refrigerate for up to 1 day. Makes about 10 oz. —*JS*

● STRONG ● SWEET ◐ TART ● BITTER ● FRUITY ● HERBAL ● SMOKY ● SPICY

MAGNETIC POLE
REVERSAL

COY ROY

Makes **1** ●●○○○○○○○○

Shannon Ponche, mixologist at Mayahuel in New York City, describes this tequila cocktail as "robust and boozy, kind of like a twist on a Sazerac." She gives it a great sweet-tart flavor with maple syrup and apple cider vinegar.

¾ tsp. pure maple syrup
¾ tsp. apple cider vinegar
1 oz. reposado tequila, preferably El Tesoro
½ oz. Jamaican rum
½ oz. rye whiskey
½ oz. Velvet Falernum (clove-spiced liqueur)
2 dashes of Angostura bitters
Ice
1 grapefruit twist, for garnish

In a mixing glass, stir the maple syrup with the vinegar until combined. Add the tequila, rum, rye, Velvet Falernum and bitters. Fill the glass with ice, stir well and strain into a chilled rocks glass. Pinch the grapefruit twist over the drink and add to the glass. —*Shannon Ponche*

MUM'S THE WORD

Makes **1** ●●●●●●●●

Shannon Ponche describes Mum's the Word as "floral and indulgent but easy-drinking." The herbal liqueur Bénédictine gives the cocktail a lovely honey flavor.

¼ oz. absinthe
1½ oz. French blanc vermouth, such as Dolin
¾ oz. Suze (bittersweet gentian aperitif)
½ oz. Bénédictine (spiced herbal liqueur)
½ oz. mezcal
2 dashes of orange bitters
Ice
1 lemon twist

Rinse a chilled coupe with the absinthe; pour out the excess. In a mixing glass, combine the vermouth, Suze, Bénédictine, mezcal and bitters. Fill the glass with ice, stir well and strain into the prepared coupe. Pinch the lemon twist over the drink and discard. —*Shannon Ponche*

● STRONG ● SWEET ● TART ● BITTER ● FRUITY ● HERBAL ● SMOKY ● SPICY

TO ALLEVIATE APPARENT DEATH

Makes **1** ●●●●●●●●●

Time **5 min plus 3 days for infusing the tequila**

"Sometimes I fixate on an ingredient and really want to work with it," says Chicago mixologist Jay Schroeder. "One day, I was determined to feature cocoa beans in a cocktail." He steeps dark cocoa nibs in tequila to give this drink a deep chocolate flavor, while guajillo chile adds a lingering heat.

One ½-inch-long piece of guajillo chile
Scant ½ tsp. Simple Syrup (p. 37)
2 oz. Dark Cocoa Tequila (below)
½ oz. Carpano Antica Formula or other sweet vermouth
¼ oz. walnut liqueur, preferably Nux Alpina
Ice
1 orange twist, for garnish

In a mixing glass, muddle the chile with the Simple Syrup. Add the Dark Cocoa Tequila, vermouth and walnut liqueur. Fill the glass with ice, stir well and fine-strain (p. 27) into a chilled coupe. Pinch the orange twist over the drink and add to the coupe. —*Jay Schroeder*

DARK COCOA TEQUILA
In a jar, muddle ¼ tsp. dark cocoa nibs with ¼ oz. añejo tequila (preferably Chinaco) until the nibs are finely crushed. Add 6 oz. tequila, cover the jar and let stand at room temperature for 3 days, shaking the jar once a day. Pour the infused tequila through a fine strainer and keep at room temperature for up to 1 month. Makes about 6 oz. —*JS*

PASTORELA

Makes **1** ●●●●●●●●●

Time **5 min plus steeping the syrup**

Jay Schroeder created this beer-and-tequila cocktail for Frontera Grill in Chicago. He sweetens it with a syrup made from panela, a dark, molasses-y Latin American sugar (known as piloncillo in Mexico). Schroeder spices the syrup with cloves and ginger–"flavors that remind me of baking with my mother at Christmastime," he says.

4 oz. Negra Modelo beer
1 oz. añejo tequila
1 oz. Panela Syrup (below)
¾ oz. fresh lime juice
    Ice
1 orange twist, preferably spiral-cut (p. 26), for garnish

Pour the beer into a large chilled wineglass. In a cocktail shaker, combine the tequila, Panela Syrup and lime juice. Fill the shaker with ice and shake well. Strain into the wineglass and garnish with the orange twist. *—Jay Schroeder*

PANELA SYRUP

In a medium saucepan, combine 10 oz. chopped dark panela (a.k.a. piloncillo or unrefined cane sugar), ⅓ cup peeled and chopped fresh ginger, ⅔ cup water, 2 tsp. ancho powder, 1¼ tsp. whole cloves and the zest from 1 orange. Simmer over moderately low heat, stirring occasionally, until the panela is dissolved and the syrup is very fragrant, about 7 minutes. Let cool, then pour through a fine strainer into a jar. If desired, strain the syrup again through cheesecloth to remove any residual ancho powder. Refrigerate for up to 2 weeks. Makes about 8 oz. *—JS*

● STRONG ● SWEET ● TART ● BITTER ● FRUITY ● HERBAL ● SMOKY ● SPICY

PASTORELA

SAGE ADVICE

Makes **1**

"This is a great summertime drink," says Shannon Ponche, bartender at Mayahuel in New York City. It's an herbal twist on a caipirinha, using fresh sage leaves and crema de mezcal (a blend of mezcal and sweet agave syrup).

3 **lime wedges**
1 **oz. crema de mezcal**
1 **oz. cachaça**
¼ **oz. Rich Simple Syrup (p. 37)**
4 **sage leaves**
3 **ice cubes, plus crushed ice (p. 27) for serving**

In a cocktail shaker, muddle 2 of the lime wedges. Add the crema de mezcal, cachaça, Rich Simple Syrup, 3 of the sage leaves and the 3 ice cubes and shake well. Pour into a chilled rocks glass, fill the glass with crushed ice and garnish with the remaining lime wedge and sage leaf. —*Shannon Ponche*

ALL QUIET

Makes **1**

Inspired by perfumers, Chicago mixologist Jay Schroeder adds a drop of neroli oil to this cocktail. Extracted from bitter-orange blossoms, "it's got that wonderful, bright, floral aroma that's very welcoming and warming," he says. The drink is fabulous without neroli oil, too.

1½ **oz. blanco sotol (grassy Mexican spirit), preferably Ocho Cientos**
½ **oz. Lillet blanc**
¼ **oz. Amaro Montenegro**
1 **drop of neroli oil (optional; see Note)**
  Ice
1 **orange twist, for garnish**

In a mixing glass, combine the sotol, Lillet, amaro and neroli oil. Fill the glass with ice, stir well and strain into a chilled coupe. Pinch the orange twist over the drink and add to the coupe. —*Jay Schroeder*

Note Neroli oil is available at health food stores and from *amazon.com*.

● STRONG ● SWEET ○ TART ● BITTER ● FRUITY ● HERBAL ● SMOKY ● SPICY

SAGE ADVICE

SMOKE SHOW

Makes **1**

This refreshing cocktail gets its sweetness from pomegranate molasses (available at Middle Eastern markets) and intensely raisiny Moscatel sherry.

- 1 **oz. mezcal**
- 1 **oz. Moscatel sherry**
- ¾ **oz. fresh lemon juice**
- ½ **oz. Simple Syrup (p. 37)**
- 1 **tsp. pomegranate molasses**
  Ice

In a cocktail shaker, combine the mezcal, sherry, lemon juice, Simple Syrup and pomegranate molasses. Fill the shaker with ice, shake well and strain into a chilled coupe. —*Shannon Ponche*

CLASSIC

ROSITA

Makes **1**

Cocktail historian Gary Regan (of Regan's bitters) rediscovered this drink when a friend asked him about its origin. While researching the recipe, Regan realized that he himself had written it up in his 1991 book, The Bartender's Bible.

- 1½ **oz. reposado tequila**
- ½ **oz. dry vermouth**
- ½ **oz. sweet vermouth**
- ½ **oz. Campari**
  Dash of Angostura bitters
  Ice

In a mixing glass, combine the tequila, vermouths, Campari and bitters. Fill two-thirds of the mixing glass with ice and stir well. Strain into a chilled martini glass.

● STRONG　● SWEET　● TART　● BITTER　● FRUITY　● HERBAL　● SMOKY　● SPICY

PALOMA

Makes **1** ●●●●●●●●●●

Noted mixologist Philip Ward combines fresh grapefruit juice, simple syrup and club soda to make his own grapefruit soda for this recipe. Alternatively, you can swap in a good-quality soda like San Pellegrino Pompelmo.

📷 p. 90

2   **lime wedges and kosher salt**
2   **oz. blanco tequila**
1   **oz. fresh grapefruit juice**
¾   **oz. fresh lime juice**
½   **oz. Simple Syrup (p. 37)**
     Ice
1   **oz. chilled club soda**

Moisten the outer rim of a chilled highball glass with 1 lime wedge and coat lightly with salt. In a cocktail shaker, combine the tequila, grapefruit juice, lime juice and Simple Syrup. Fill the shaker with ice and shake well. Strain into the prepared glass, stir in the club soda and garnish with the remaining lime wedge.

MARGARITA

Makes **1** ●●●●●●●●●●

Arguably the most popular cocktail in the United States, the margarita is said to have been invented in the 1930s by the manager of the Garci Crespo Hotel in Puebla, Mexico. His girlfriend, Margarita, loved salt with her drinks.

2   **lime wedges and kosher salt**
2   **oz. blanco tequila**
¾   **oz. Cointreau or other triple sec**
¾   **oz. fresh lime juice**
¼   **oz. Simple Syrup (p. 37)**
     Ice

Moisten half of the outer rim of a chilled coupe with 1 lime wedge and coat lightly with salt. In a cocktail shaker, combine the tequila, Cointreau, lime juice and Simple Syrup. Fill the shaker with ice and shake well. Strain into the prepared coupe and garnish with the remaining lime wedge.

● STRONG ● SWEET ● TART ● BITTER ● FRUITY ● HERBAL ● SMOKY ● SPICY

EL DIABLO

Makes **1** ⚫⚫⚫⚫⚫⚫⚫⚫⚫⚫

The provenance of this classic is hard to pin down. One verifiable fact: It appeared in Trader Vic's 1947 Bartender's Guide as the Mexican El Diablo and was one of the first tequila cocktails.

3	oz. chilled ginger beer
1½	oz. blanco tequila
½	oz. crème de cassis (black-currant liqueur)
½	oz. fresh lime juice
	Ice
1	lime wheel, for garnish

In a chilled collins glass, combine the ginger beer, tequila, crème de cassis and lime juice. Fill the glass with ice and stir well. Garnish with the lime wheel.

RED SANGRITA

Makes **6** ⚫⚫⚫⚫⚫⚫⚫⚫⚫

Time **20 min plus chilling**

In Mexico, this spicy, citrusy tomato drink is the traditional chaser to sip with good tequila.

15	oz. tomato juice
7	oz. fresh orange juice
3	oz. fresh grapefruit juice
2	oz. hot sauce
1¼	oz. fresh lime juice
½	jalapeño (with seeds for a spicier drink)
1½	tsp. pepper
1	tsp. salt
	About 9 oz. blanco tequila

In a large pitcher, combine all of the ingredients except the tequila and stir until the salt is dissolved. Let stand for 15 minutes (30 minutes for a spicier drink). Discard the jalapeño and refrigerate the sangrita until chilled, about 2 hours. Stir well and pour into rocks glasses. Serve with shots of tequila alongside.

LAST LOVE LETTER, P. 108

APERITIFS
VODKA
GIN
TEQUILA
RUM
WHISKEY
BRANDY
NIGHTCAPS
BIG BATCH
MOCKTAILS

EYEBALL KID

Makes **1** ●●○○○○○○○○

Time **5 min plus
1 day for infusing
the orgeat**

*Sara Justice is the
head bartender at The
Franklin Mortgage
& Investment Co.,
a speakeasy-style bar
in Philadelphia. She
stumbled across
heirloom benne seeds
(sesame seeds) when
she lived in Georgia
and thought they'd
be a great savory
addition to a cocktail,
so she infused them
into orgeat. "I love
playing around with
nuts and seeds in
drinks, especially
since my grandfather
was raised by
millers," she says.*

1	oz. white rum, preferably Botran Reserva Blanca
¾	oz. Benne Seed Orgeat (below) or orgeat (almond-flavored syrup)
¾	oz. fresh lemon juice
½	oz. genever
½	oz. aquavit
	Ice

In a cocktail shaker, combine the rum, Benne Seed Orgeat, lemon juice, genever and aquavit. Fill the shaker with ice and shake well. Strain into a chilled coupe. —*Sara Justice*

BENNE SEED ORGEAT

In a small skillet, toast ¼ cup benne seeds (a.k.a. sesame seeds) over low heat until fragrant, about 4 minutes. Transfer the seeds to a blender, add 6 oz. water and blend at low speed until combined, about 30 seconds. Transfer to a jar, cover and let stand for 24 hours. Strain the seeds out and discard. Return the liquid to the jar (you should have about 4 oz.) and add ½ cup Demerara sugar and ¾ tsp. orange flower water. Cover and shake the jar vigorously to combine. Refrigerate for up to 3 weeks. Makes about 6 oz. —*SJ*

● STRONG ● SWEET ○ TART ● BITTER ● FRUITY ● HERBAL ● SMOKY ● SPICY

CROSS-EYED AND PAINLESS

Makes **1** ●●●●●●●●●

Time **5 min plus steeping the rum**

Philadelphia bartender Sara Justice was fascinated by a fact she discovered in the best-selling Drunken Botanist: "Olives and jasmine are in the same plant family, so I thought it would be fun to do a martini variation with jasmine."

- 2 oz. Jasmine Green Tea Rum (below)
- 1 oz. amontillado sherry
- 1 teaspoon crème de noyaux (almond-flavored liqueur)
  Ice
- 1 brined green olive, such as Arbequina, skewered on a pick, for garnish

In a mixing glass, combine the Jasmine Green Tea Rum, sherry and crème de noyaux. Fill the glass with ice and stir well. Strain into a chilled coupe and garnish with the skewered olive.
—*Sara Justice*

JASMINE GREEN TEA RUM

In a liquid measuring cup, combine 8 oz. white rum with 1 Tbsp. loose jasmine green tea and let steep for 30 minutes. Strain into a jar and refrigerate for up to 2 weeks. Makes about 8 oz. —*SJ*

LAST LOVE LETTER

Makes **1** ●●●●●●●●

"My friends say that even though I'm not sad, I'm in love with the idea of being sad," says Colin O'Neill, bartender at Oyster House in Philadelphia. "The Last Love Letter is a rich, sultry cocktail to sip while contemplating lost loves and forgotten promises."

 p. 104

- 1 oz. aged Demerara rum, preferably El Dorado 8-year
- ½ oz. dark rum, such as Gosling's
- ½ oz. Jamaican amber rum, such as Appleton V/X
- 1 tsp. Rich Simple Syrup (p. 37)
- 8 drops of tiki bitters
  Dash of orange bitters
  Ice, plus 1 large cube for serving
- 1 orange twist, for garnish

In a mixing glass, combine the rums, Rich Simple Syrup and both bitters. Fill the glass with ice, stir well and strain into a chilled rocks glass over the large ice cube. Pinch the orange twist over the drink and add to the glass. —*Colin O'Neill*

● STRONG ● SWEET ● TART ● BITTER ● FRUITY ● HERBAL ● SMOKY ● SPICY

PSYCHEDELIC JUNGLE

Makes **1** ●●●●●●●●

While taking wine-tasting classes, Philadelphia mixologist Sara Justice became obsessed with Beaujolais. "It has these strawberry and banana flavors that I thought would be delicious in a rum cocktail," she says.

For a mocktail variation, see p. 200.

One ⅛-inch-thick slice of jalapeño (with seeds)
¾ oz. Raspberry Syrup (p. 78)
1 oz. Jamaican white rum, preferably Plantation 3 Stars
¾ oz. fresh lime juice
½ oz. Beaujolais wine
½ oz. Zucca (rhubarb-flavored amaro)
½ tsp. banana liqueur
Ice

In a cocktail shaker, lightly muddle the jalapeño with the Raspberry Syrup. Add the rum, lime juice, wine, Zucca and banana liqueur. Fill the shaker with ice and shake well. Fine-strain (p. 27) into a chilled coupe. —*Sara Justice*

MR. PALOMAR

Makes **1** ●●●●●●●●

In this Negroni variation, Sara Justice replaces the usual gin with rhum agricole. "It's made from fresh-cut sugarcane and has a very grassy flavor," she says. Before serving, she sprinkles sea salt on the ice cubes to temper the bitterness.

1 oz. white rhum agricole
1 oz. Gran Classico Bitter (bittersweet herbal liqueur)
1 oz. Cocchi Americano Rosa (rose-colored, slightly bitter aperitif wine)
9 drops of tiki bitters
Ice
Pinch of sea salt
½ orange wheel, for garnish

In a mixing glass, combine the rhum agricole, Gran Classico Bitter, Cocchi Americano and bitters. Fill the glass with ice and stir well. Strain into a chilled, ice-filled rocks glass. Sprinkle the salt onto the ice and garnish with the orange wheel. —*Sara Justice*

● STRONG ● SWEET ● TART ● BITTER ● FRUITY ● HERBAL ● SMOKY ● SPICY

JUST CAUSE

Makes **1** ●●●●●●●●●

"This drink is like a crazy, tropical French 75," says Chicago-based mixologist Alex Renshaw. He replaces the gin in the classic with cachaça and Chareau, an aloe vera liqueur with a minty, cucumber taste. If Chareau isn't available, substitute aloe vera juice from a health food store or juice bar.

Five 1-inch cubes of cantaloupe
1½ oz. cachaça, preferably Novo Fogo Silver
¾ oz. fresh lemon juice
⅔ oz. Simple Syrup (p. 37)
¼ oz. aloe vera liqueur or juice
     Dash of fennel bitters
     Ice
1 oz. chilled Prosecco
1 mint leaf, smacked (p. 27), for garnish

In a cocktail shaker, muddle the cantaloupe. Add the cachaça, lemon juice, Simple Syrup, aloe vera liqueur and bitters. Fill the shaker with ice and shake well. Strain into a chilled flute and top with the Prosecco. Clap the mint leaf between your hands over the cocktail to release the essential oils and add to the glass.
—*Alex Renshaw*

HONOR AMONGST THIEVES

Makes **1** ●●●●●●●●●

This is Alex Renshaw's take on a tiki cocktail. "It's essentially a sour that I broke the rules with," he says. Renshaw sweetens the sugarcane-based cachaça and bourbon with pineapple juice and citrusy Velvet Falernum.

1 oz. aged cachaça, preferably Novo Fogo
1 oz. 100-proof bourbon, such as Old Forester Signature
1 oz. unsweetened pineapple juice
½ oz. Velvet Falernum (clove-spiced liqueur)
¼ oz. fresh lime juice
¼ oz. Simple Syrup (p. 37)
     Ice, plus 1 large cube for serving
3 dashes of Peychaud's bitters, for garnish

In a cocktail shaker, combine the cachaça, bourbon, pineapple juice, Velvet Falernum, lime juice and Simple Syrup. Fill the shaker with ice and shake well. Strain into a chilled rocks glass over the large ice cube and garnish with the bitters. —*Alex Renshaw*

● STRONG ● SWEET ○ TART ● BITTER ● FRUITY ● HERBAL ● SMOKY ● SPICY

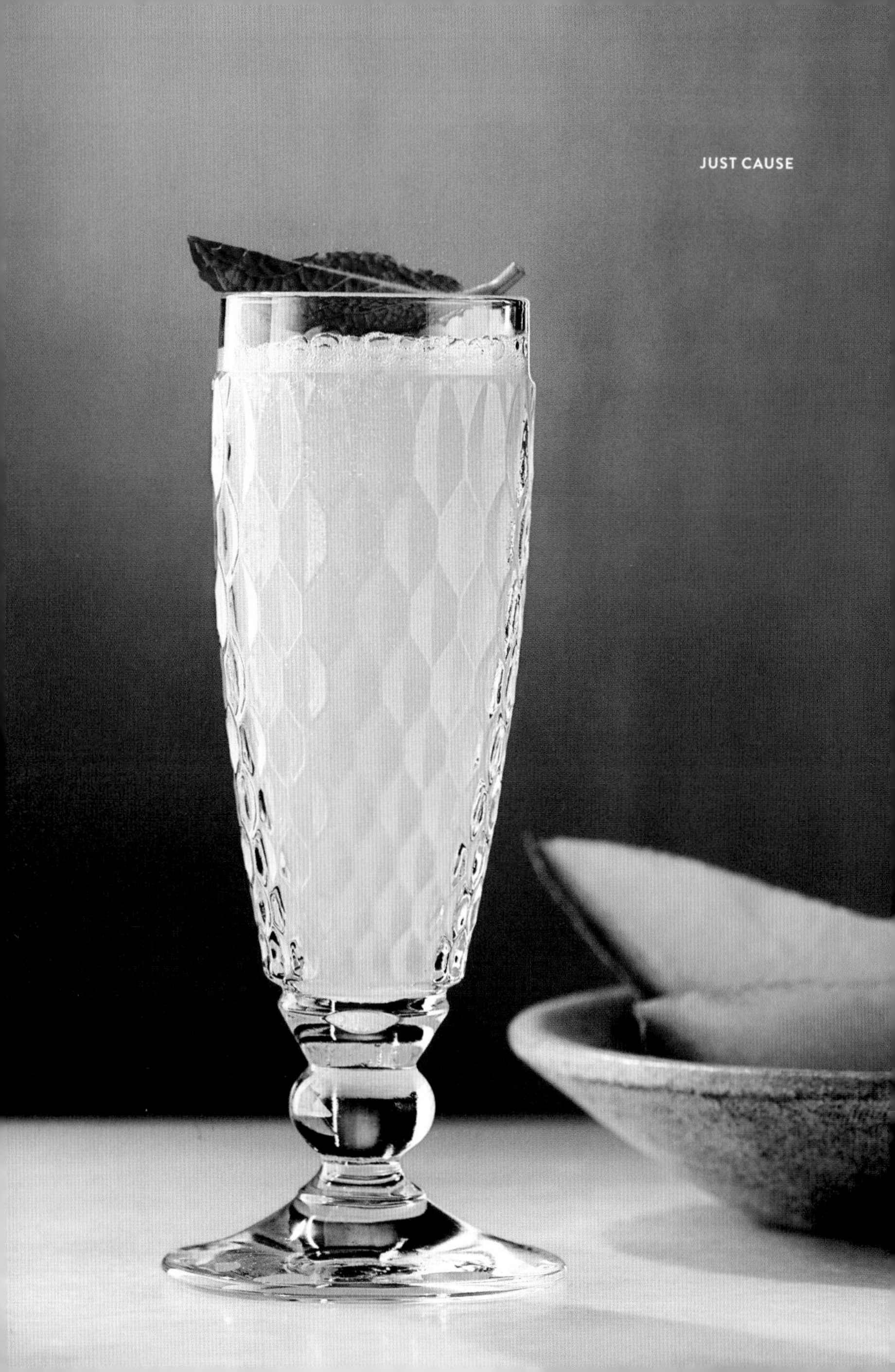

SIR GREENDOWN PUNCH

Makes **1** ●●●●●●●●●
Time **10 min**

*Philadelphia
mixologist Colin
O'Neill loves creating
syrups, then
brainstorming spirits
to go with them.
Here, he uses a chai
tea syrup to sweeten
and spice punch. The
recipe is for a single
serving but can be
easily multiplied to
make a big batch.*

- 1 oz. aged rhum agricole
- 1 oz. VS Cognac, preferably Landy
- 1 oz. Chai Tea Syrup (below)
- ¾ oz. fresh lemon juice
- ½ oz. fresh grapefruit juice
- 1 tsp. Velvet Falernum (clove-spiced liqueur)
    Ice
    Pinch of freshly grated nutmeg, for garnish

In a chilled wineglass, combine the rum, Cognac, Chai Tea Syrup, lemon juice, grapefruit juice and Velvet Falernum. Fill the glass with ice and stir well. Garnish with the nutmeg. —*Colin O'Neill*

CHAI TEA SYRUP

In heatproof jar, steep 2 Tbsp. loose chai tea in 8 oz. boiling water for 4 minutes. Strain the tea. Add ¾ cup Demerara sugar, cover and shake until fully dissolved. Refrigerate for up to 3 weeks. Makes about 10 oz. —*CO*

IRONSIDE

Makes **1** ●●●●●●●●●

*Cachaça is most
often associated
with citrusy
caipirinhas. Here,
Alex Renshaw
incorporates the
sugarcane spirit
in a rich, sweet
and tropical after-
dinner drink.*

- 1 oz. cachaça, such as Leblon
- 1 oz. Cardamaro (wine-based amaro)
- ½ oz. banana liqueur, such as Briottet
- ½ oz. Moscatel sherry, such as Lustau
- 2 dashes of Angostura bitters
    Ice
- 1 lemon twist

In a mixing glass, combine the cachaça, Cardamaro, banana liqueur, sherry and bitters. Fill the glass with ice, stir well and strain into a chilled coupe. Pinch the lemon twist over the drink and discard. —*Alex Renshaw*

● STRONG ● SWEET ● TART ● BITTER ● FRUITY ● HERBAL ● SMOKY ● SPICY

SIR GREENDOWN PUNCH

THE GRAVITRON

Makes **1** ●●○○○○○○○○

"This is a really playful, effervescent drink," says Colin O'Neill of Philadelphia's Oyster House. *"The peach and cinnamon are so familiar and so fun with crème de cacao."*

Two ¼-inch-thick slices of peach
½ oz. Cinnamon Syrup (p. 70)
1¼ oz. Jamaican rum, preferably Appleton V/X
¾ oz. Cocchi Americano Rosa (rose-colored, slightly bitter aperitif wine)
¾ oz. fresh lemon juice
¼ oz. white crème de cacao
Dash of Peychaud's bitters
Dash of Jerry Thomas bitters
Ice
1½ oz. chilled brut Prosecco

In a cocktail shaker, muddle the peach with the Cinnamon Syrup. Add the rum, Cocchi Americano, lemon juice, crème de cacao and both bitters. Fill the shaker with ice and shake well. Fine-strain (p. 27) into a chilled, ice-filled collins glass and top with the Prosecco. —*Colin O'Neill*

ZING! WENT THE STRINGS OF MY HEART

Makes **1** ●○●○○●○○○

Colin O'Neill created this lush, nutty dessert cocktail for a Valentine's Day menu. "I've always liked decadent and sort of sweet drinks," he says. *"It's not really a guilty pleasure because I'm not ashamed of it at all."*

2 oz. aged rum, preferably Barbancourt 4-year
½ oz. Raspberry Syrup (p. 78)
½ oz. heavy cream
¼ oz. Frangelico
Dash of chocolate bitters
1 large egg
Ice
1 raspberry and finely grated dark chocolate, for garnish

In a cocktail shaker, combine the rum, Raspberry Syrup, cream, Frangelico, bitters and egg; shake vigorously. Fill the shaker with ice and shake again. Strain into a chilled coupe and garnish with the raspberry and chocolate. —*Colin O'Neill*

● STRONG ● SWEET ○ TART ● BITTER ● FRUITY ◉ HERBAL ● SMOKY ● SPICY

BEG YOUR PARDON

Makes **1** ⬤⬤⬤⬤⬤⬤◦◦◦
Time **5 min plus 1 day for infusing the Chartreuse**

"I wanted to create a spicy, refreshing drink that would showcase cachaça in a different way," says Chicago's Alex Renshaw. Here, he mixes cachaça with jalapeño-infused Chartreuse.

¾ oz. cachaça, preferably Novo Fogo Silver
¾ oz. Jalapeño Chartreuse (below)
¾ oz. maraschino liqueur
¾ oz. fresh lemon juice
¾ oz. unsweetened pineapple juice
1 cilantro sprig, plus 1 cilantro leaf, smacked (p. 27), for garnish
Ice

In a cocktail shaker, combine the cachaça, Jalapeño Chartreuse, maraschino liqueur, lemon juice, pineapple juice and cilantro sprig. Fill the shaker with ice and shake well. Fine-strain (p. 27) into a chilled coupe and garnish with the smacked cilantro leaf. —*Alex Renshaw*

JALAPEÑO CHARTREUSE

In a jar, combine 8 oz. green Chartreuse with 1 Tbsp. chopped jalapeño (about ½ small jalapeño) and let stand for 24 hours. Strain the infused Chartreuse and refrigerate for up to 2 weeks. Makes about 8 oz. —*AR*

CLASSIC

DARK AND STORMY

Makes **1** ◦◦◦⬤⬤⬤⬤⬤⬤

Per Gosling's lore, this drink was invented more than 100 years ago when members of Bermuda's Royal Naval Officer's Club added a splash of the local rum to their ginger beer.

2 oz. dark rum, preferably Gosling's
½ oz. fresh lime juice (optional)
Ice
3 oz. chilled ginger beer
1 lime wheel, for garnish

In a cocktail shaker, combine the rum and lime juice. Fill the shaker with ice and shake well. Strain into a chilled, ice-filled collins glass, stir in the ginger beer and garnish with the lime wheel.

CLASSIC

QUEEN'S PARK SWIZZLE

Makes **1** ⬤⬤⬤⬤⬤⬤⬤⬤⬤

This early-1900s lime-rum cocktail was born at Trinidad's now-closed Queen's Park Hotel. It is traditionally served over crushed ice and mixed with a swizzle stick.

- 2 oz. aged Demerara rum, such as El Dorado 15-year
- 1 oz. fresh lime juice
- ½ oz. Rich Simple Syrup (p. 37)
  Crushed ice (p. 27) or pebble ice (slightly larger and more rounded than crushed ice)
- 2 dashes of Angostura bitters
- 2 dashes of Peychaud's bitters
- 1 mint sprig, for garnish

In a chilled collins glass, combine the rum, lime juice and Rich Simple Syrup. Fill the glass with crushed ice and spin a swizzle stick or bar spoon between your hands to mix the drink, then add more crushed ice. Top with both bitters and garnish with the mint sprig.

CLASSIC

MOJITO

Makes **1** ⬤⬤⬤⬤⬤⬤⬤⬤⬤

The oldest-known recipe for the mojito appeared as the Mojo de Ron in a 1929 Cuban guide called Libro de Cocktail (The Cocktail Book).

- 5 mint leaves, plus 1 mint sprig for garnish
- 1½ oz. chilled club soda
  Ice
- 1½ oz. white rum
- ¾ oz. fresh lime juice
- ¾ oz. Simple Syrup (p. 37)

In a chilled collins glass, muddle the mint leaves with ½ oz. of the soda. Fill the glass with ice. In a cocktail shaker, combine the rum, lime juice and Simple Syrup. Fill the shaker with ice and shake well. Strain into the prepared glass, stir in the remaining soda and garnish with the mint sprig.

⬤ STRONG ⬤ SWEET ◯ TART ⬤ BITTER ⬤ FRUITY ⬤ HERBAL ⬤ SMOKY ⬤ SPICY

MAI TAI

Makes **1** ●●○○○○○○○

Victor "Trader Vic" Bergeron created the mai tai in 1944 using a private stash of 17-year-old imported Jamaican rum. This recipe uses a blend of aged rums to approximate its flavor.

1   oz. aged dark rum, preferably Jamaican
1   oz. aged Martinique rum, such as Rhum J.M
¾   oz. fresh lime juice, lime shell (half lime, juiced and turned inside out) reserved for garnish
½   oz. orange curaçao
½   oz. orgeat (almond-flavored syrup)
    Crushed ice (p. 27)
    1 mint sprig and 1 pineapple spear (optional), for garnish

In a cocktail shaker, combine both rums, the lime juice, curaçao and orgeat. Fill the shaker with crushed ice and shake well. Pour into a chilled double rocks or hurricane glass and garnish with the lime shell, mint sprig and pineapple spear.

HEMINGWAY DAIQUIRI

Makes **1** ○○●○○○○○○

Ernest Hemingway once wrote that daiquiris "felt, as you drank them, the way downhill glacier-skiing feels running through powder snow." The daiquiri that Hemingway liked best included grapefruit juice and maraschino liqueur.

2   oz. white rum
¾   oz. fresh lime juice
½   oz. fresh grapefruit juice
½   oz. maraschino liqueur
    Ice
1   lime wheel, for garnish (optional)

In a cocktail shaker, combine the rum, lime and grapefruit juices and maraschino liqueur. Fill the shaker with ice and shake well. Strain into a chilled coupe and garnish with the lime wheel.

● STRONG ● SWEET ○ TART ● BITTER ● FRUITY ● HERBAL ● SMOKY ● SPICY

BLOOD AND SAND (LEFT), P. 148
THE YUBARI KING, P. 125

APERITIFS

VODKA

GIN

TEQUILA

RUM

WHISKEY

BRANDY

NIGHTCAPS

BIG BATCH

MOCKTAILS

CHARLESTON SOUR

Makes **1** ●●●●●●●●●

Time **5 min plus infusing the vinegar**

In this tribute to his hometown, Charleston mixologist Ryan Casey of Edmund's Oast uses a DIY pineapple vinegar. "Pineapples are all over Charleston...on people's gates and on a big fountain downtown," he says. The pineapple became an international symbol of hospitality back in Colonial times when seafaring captains would return home from the Caribbean and spike a pineapple on their gate–a signal to neighbors that they were welcome to visit.

For a mocktail variation, see p. 196.

1¾ oz. bourbon, preferably Bulleit
½ oz. Pineapple Vinegar (below)
½ oz. fresh lemon juice
½ oz. Simple Syrup (p. 37)
    Ice
¼ oz. Sercial Madeira

In a cocktail shaker, combine the bourbon, Pineapple Vinegar, lemon juice and Simple Syrup. Fill the shaker with ice, shake well and strain into a chilled, ice-filled highball glass. Float the Madeira on top, slowly pouring it over the back of a bar spoon near the drink's surface. *—Ryan Casey*

PINEAPPLE VINEGAR

In a medium saucepan, simmer 4 oz. unsweetened pineapple juice over high heat until reduced by half, about 7 minutes. Remove from the heat and stir in 6 oz. white vinegar and ¼ cup sugar. Let stand until the sugar completely dissolves, about 10 minutes. Pour the infused vinegar into a jar and refrigerate for up to 3 weeks. Makes about 9 oz. *—RC*

● STRONG ● SWEET ○ TART ● BITTER ● FRUITY ● HERBAL ● SMOKY ● SPICY

THE YUBARI KING

Makes **1** ⬤⬤⬤⬤⬤⬤⬤⬤⬤⬤

Jason Patz, bartender at Denver's Williams & Graham, named this drink after the luxury Japanese melon prized for its sweet orange flesh and perfectly round shape. (A pair can fetch up to $21,000 at auction.) Patz shakes cubes of cantaloupe with Nikka Yoichi whisky from Hokkaido, also the birthplace of Yubari King melons.

📷 p. 122

Four 1-inch cantaloupe cubes, plus 1 or 2 cantaloupe balls skewered on a pick for garnish
2 oz. 12-year Japanese whisky or Nikka Yoichi 15-year
½ oz. Simple Syrup (p. 37)
½ oz. fresh lemon juice
Ice

In a cocktail shaker, muddle the cantaloupe cubes. Add the whisky, Simple Syrup and lemon juice. Fill the shaker with ice and shake well. Fine-strain (p. 27) into a chilled double rocks glass and garnish with the skewered melon balls. —*Jason Patz*

EVERGREEN TERRACE

Makes **1** ⬤⬤⬤⬤⬤⬤⬤⬤⬤⬤

This bright, bitter-sweet bourbon cocktail is named for the street where the TV family the Simpsons live. "Anyone who gets the reference loves it," says Ryan Casey.

2 oz. bourbon, preferably Johnny Drum Private Stock
¾ oz. Campari
½ oz. Strega (Italian herbal liqueur)
¼ oz. ginger liqueur
Ice

In a mixing glass, combine the bourbon, Campari, Strega and ginger liqueur. Fill the glass with ice and stir for 30 seconds. Let rest for 30 seconds, then strain into a chilled coupe. —*Ryan Casey*

SERGIO LEONE

Makes 1

Charleston bartender Ryan Casey sprinkles piment d'Espelette (Basque smoked paprika) on the large ice cubes in this cocktail. "If you want just a little Espelette in the drink, leave the ice alone," he says. "If you want to spice it up, knock the ice over and stir."

1¼ oz. bourbon, preferably Basil Hayden's
1   oz. Suze (bittersweet gentian aperitif)
¾   oz. French blanc vermouth, such as Dolin
    Ice, plus 2 large cubes for serving
    Pinch of piment d'Espelette, for garnish

In a mixing glass, combine the bourbon, Suze and vermouth. Fill the glass with ice and stir for 30 seconds. Let rest for 30 seconds, then strain into a chilled highball glass over the large ice cubes. Sprinkle the piment d'Espelette on the ice. —Ryan Casey

MARK THE BIRD

Makes 1 ○○○○○○○○●

Manuka honey, from the New Zealand manuka bush, sweetens this sour-style drink. "Manuka has this crazy, leathery thing going on," says Chris Elford of Rob Roy in Seattle. "It adds another level of flavor–like spices in cooking." Manuka honey is available at health food stores and amazon.com. You can also use another dark honey like buckwheat.

1½ oz. rye whiskey
½   oz. fresh lemon juice
½   oz. dark honey syrup (¼ oz. dark honey,
    such as buckwheat or manuka, mixed with
    ¼ oz. hot water and cooled)
    Pinch of cayenne pepper
    Ice
1   oz. chilled Prosecco

In a cocktail shaker, combine the rye, lemon juice, honey syrup and cayenne. Fill the shaker with ice and shake well. Strain into a chilled coupe or Champagne flute and top with the Prosecco.
—Chris Elford

● STRONG ● SWEET ○ TART ● BITTER ● FRUITY ● HERBAL ● SMOKY ● SPICY

SERGIO LEONE

MATCHA HIGHBALL

Makes **1** ⦿⦿⦿⦿⦿⦿⦿⦿

A trip to Japan inspired Denver bartender Jason Patz to combine matcha (a vivid green-tea powder) with Japanese whisky. Matcha tends to clump when mixed with liquid; to loosen any that's stuck to the side of the shaker, swirl the club soda in the shaker before pouring it into the glass.

2 oz. 12-year Japanese whisky, preferably Hibiki
½ oz. fresh lemon juice
½ oz. Honey Syrup (p. 37)
¼ tsp. matcha green-tea powder
   Ice
4 oz. chilled club soda
1 lemon wheel, for garnish

In a cocktail shaker, combine the whisky, lemon juice, Honey Syrup and matcha; shake vigorously. Pour into a chilled, ice-filled collins glass. Pour the club soda into the shaker, swirl around to rinse, then stir into the glass. Garnish with the lemon wheel. —*Jason Patz*

DURRA COCKTAIL

Makes **1** ⦿⦿⦿⦿⦿⦿⦿⦿

In this old-fashioned variation, Seattle bartender Chris Elford uses molasses-like sorghum syrup (called "durra" in northeastern Africa). According to Elford, sorghum syrup is rich and earthy and goes particularly well with spicy rye.

1½ oz. rye whiskey
½ oz. apple brandy
¼ oz. sorghum syrup (¾ tsp. sorghum syrup mixed with ¾ tsp. hot water and cooled)
1 tsp. smoky Islay Scotch, preferably Ardbeg 10-year
2 dashes of Angostura bitters
   Ice, plus 1 large cube for serving
1 orange twist and 1 to 3 brandied cherries skewered on a pick, for garnish

In a mixing glass, combine the whiskey, brandy, sorghum syrup, Scotch and bitters. Fill the glass with ice, stir well and strain into a chilled rocks glass over the large ice cube. Pinch the orange twist over the drink and drop it in, then garnish with the skewered cherries. —*Chris Elford*

⦿STRONG ⦿SWEET ⦿TART ⦿BITTER ⦿FRUITY ⦿HERBAL ⦿SMOKY ⦿SPICY

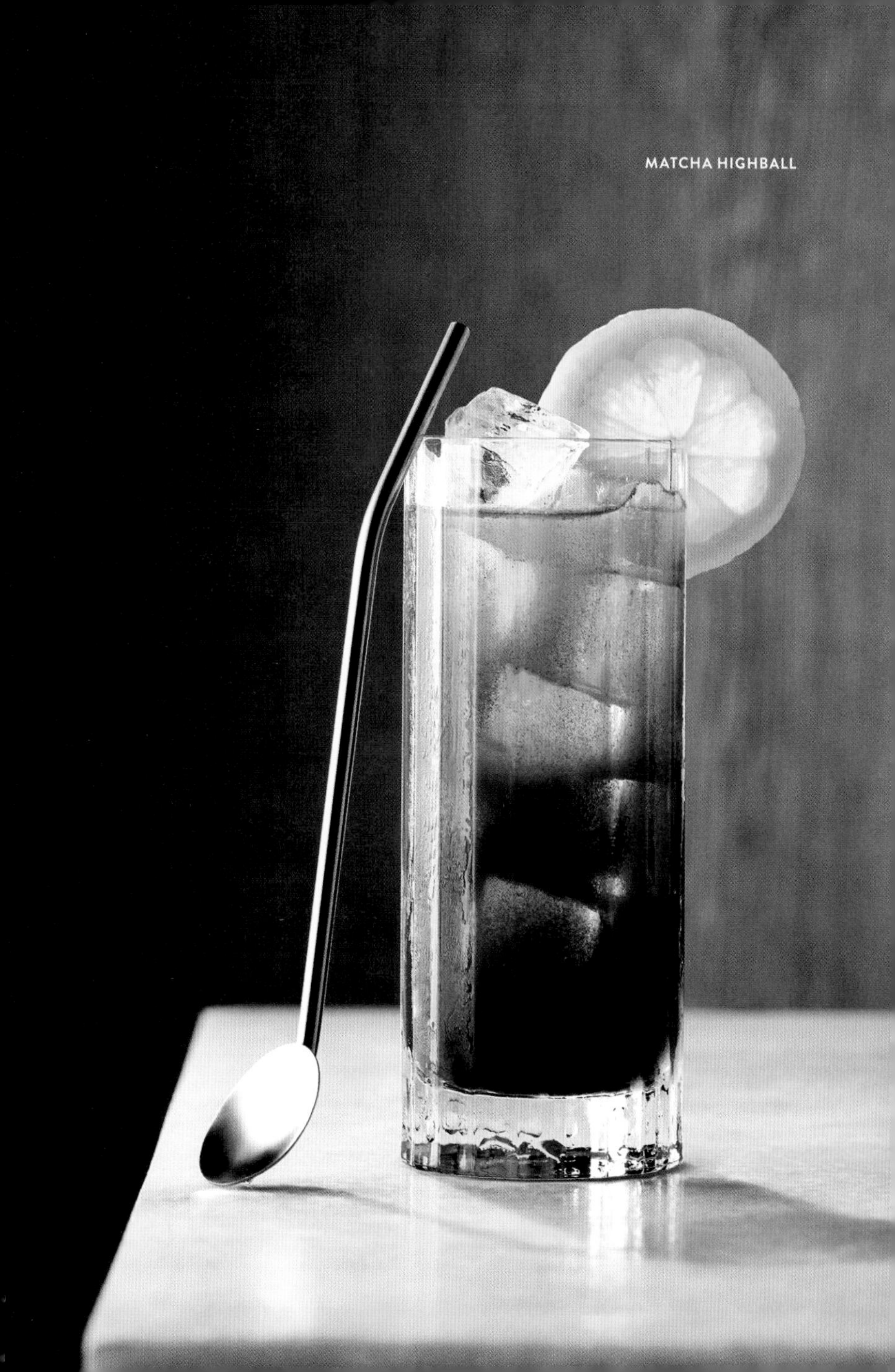

MATCHA HIGHBALL

KILT AND JACKET

Makes **1** ●●●●●●●●●

"A Tuxedo No. 2 is a delicious cocktail, but I wanted to improve on that classic," says Nick Bennett of Porchlight in New York City. In place of the gin and vermouth, he adds Highland Scotch (a typically smoky single malt, such as Glenmorangie) and nutty fino sherry.

2 oz. Highland Scotch
¾ oz. fino sherry
¼ oz. maraschino liqueur
2 dashes of orange bitters
Ice
1 brandied cherry, for garnish

In a mixing glass, combine the Scotch, sherry, maraschino liqueur and bitters. Fill the glass with ice and stir well. Strain into a chilled coupe and garnish with the cherry. —*Nick Bennett*

THE SMARTEST MAN ALIVE

Makes **1** ●●●●●●●●●

Seattle bartender Chris Elford recommends local honey for this rye cocktail. "Farmers' markets can lead you to unique honey flavors like lavender and blackberry," he says. Elford suggests making a large batch of honey syrup and adding a bit of vodka to keep the sugars from fermenting.

For a mocktail variation, see p. 202.

¾ oz. rye whiskey
¾ oz. Suze (bittersweet gentian aperitif)
¾ oz. fresh lemon juice
½ oz. Honey Syrup (p. 37)
Ice

In a cocktail shaker, combine the rye, Suze, lemon juice and Honey Syrup. Fill the shaker with ice and shake well. Fine-strain (p. 27) into a chilled coupe. —*Chris Elford*

Variation In a small saucepan, heat the ingredients over moderate heat until hot, then stir in 3 oz. brewed black tea. Pour into a warmed mug and garnish with a lemon wheel.

● STRONG ● SWEET ● TART ● BITTER ● FRUITY ● HERBAL ● SMOKY ● SPICY

ELI CASH

Makes **1** ●●●●●●●●●

This dark, rich cocktail from Charleston mixologist Ryan Casey tastes uncannily like root beer. Casey, a fan of Wes Anderson movies, named the drink after Owen Wilson's man-child character in The Royal Tenenbaums. *"It's a grown-up play on something familiar to us when we were kids," he says.*

For a mocktail variation, see p. 202.

1½ oz. bourbon, preferably Old Forester
 1 oz. Averna amaro
 ½ oz. Art in the Age root liqueur
    Dash of chocolate bitters
    Ice
 1 orange twist, for garnish

In a cocktail shaker, combine the bourbon, amaro, root liqueur and bitters. Fill the shaker with ice, shake vigorously for 30 seconds and strain into a chilled coupe. Pinch the orange twist over the drink and add to the glass. —*Ryan Casey*

LAST SONG

Makes **1** ●●●●●●●●●

"While people often drink Irish whiskey as shots, its fruity flavor is great in shaken drinks and with citrus," says Pamela Wiznitzer, bartender at Seamstress in New York City. She mixes this wonderfully spiced cocktail with apricot liqueur and cinnamon.

1¾ oz. blended Irish whiskey,
    preferably Tullamore Dew
 ¾ oz. fresh lemon juice
 ½ oz. apricot liqueur
 ⅜ oz. honey
 ⅜ oz. orgeat (almond-flavored syrup)
 3 dashes of tiki bitters
 2 pinches of ground cinnamon
    Ice

In a cocktail shaker, combine the whiskey, lemon juice, apricot liqueur, honey, orgeat, bitters and a pinch of cinnamon. Fill the shaker with ice and shake well. Strain into a chilled coupe and garnish with another pinch of cinnamon.
—*Pamela Wiznitzer*

● STRONG ● SWEET ● TART ● BITTER ● FRUITY ● HERBAL ● SMOKY ● SPICY

ELI CASH

THE ADVENTURES OF PETE AND PEACH

Makes **1**

New York City mixologist Nick Bennett combines peach brandy with a peated Scotch, shaking in egg white for a fabulous richness. The peat in the Scotch yields love-it or hate-it reactions: Comparisons range from butterscotch to Band-Aids.

For a mocktail variation, see p. 203.

- 1 oz. peated Scotch, such as Ardbeg
- 1 oz. peach brandy
- ¾ oz. fresh lemon juice
- ¾ oz. Simple Syrup (p. 37)
- 1 large egg white
-    Ice

In a cocktail shaker, combine the Scotch, peach brandy, lemon juice, Simple Syrup and egg white; shake vigorously. Fill the shaker with ice and shake again. Fine-strain (p. 27) into a chilled rocks glass. —*Nick Bennett*

11TH ROUND

Makes **1**

During a cocktail competition, New York City mixologist Pamela Wiznitzer was challenged to concoct a riff on a Rob Roy, a classic Scotch cocktail. It took her five minutes to come up with this delicious pear-and-absinthe-inflected rendition with Irish whiskey.

- 1½ oz. Irish whiskey
- ¾ oz. Cocchi Americano (fortified, slightly bitter aperitif wine)
- ½ oz. pear liqueur, such as Belle de Brillet
- ¼ oz. pear eau-de-vie
- 3 dashes of absinthe
- 3 dashes of orange bitters
-    Ice
- 1 lemon twist

In a mixing glass, combine the whiskey, Cocchi Americano, pear liqueur, eau-de-vie, absinthe and bitters. Fill the glass with ice and stir well, then strain into a chilled coupe. Pinch the lemon twist over the drink and discard. —*Pamela Wiznitzer*

● STRONG ● SWEET ○ TART ◐ BITTER ● FRUITY ● HERBAL ● SMOKY ● SPICY

THE ADVENTURES OF
PETE AND PEACH

BITTER SCOTSMAN

Makes **1** ●●●●●●●●●●

"I thought a lot about the nuances of mole for this drink," says San Diego bartender Meghan Eastman. She combines sweetness and spice with a hint of smoke in this drink, echoing the flavors of the robust Mexican sauce.

- 2 **oz. blended Scotch, such as Chivas Regal**
- ¾ **oz. orgeat (almond-flavored syrup)**
- ¾ **oz. fresh lemon juice**
- ½ **oz. Campari**
  Ice
- 1 **lemon wheel and a pinch of ground cinnamon, for garnish**

In a cocktail shaker, combine the Scotch, orgeat, lemon juice and Campari. Fill the shaker with ice and shake well. Strain into a chilled, ice-filled rocks glass and garnish with the lemon wheel and cinnamon. —*Meghan Eastman*

ITALIAN SCOT

Makes **1** ●●●●●●●●●●

"There is really nothing in a stirred cocktail that can hide any imperfections," says Meghan Eastman. "If the drink is unbalanced, you know right away." She experimented for a while with amaro and pear brandy before nailing the ratios here.

- 2 **oz. single-malt Scotch**
- ¼ **oz. Averna amaro**
- ¼ **oz. pear brandy**
- ¼ **oz. Honey Syrup (p. 37)**
- 2 **dashes of orange bitters**
  Ice
- 1 **orange twist, for garnish**

In a cocktail shaker, combine the Scotch, amaro, pear brandy, Honey Syrup and bitters. Fill the shaker with ice, shake well and strain into a chilled, ice-filled rocks glass. Pinch the orange twist over the drink and add to the glass. —*Meghan Eastman*

● STRONG ● SWEET ● TART ● BITTER ● FRUITY ● HERBAL ● SMOKY ● SPICY

BITTER SCOTSMAN

THE CIRCLE OF THE SUN

Makes **1** ●●●●●●●●●

"I was looking to make a spirituous cocktail, but one that isn't a punch-you-in-the-mouth drink," says Jason Patz, bartender at Williams & Graham in Denver. He lightens Japanese whisky with vermouth and pear liqueur in this four-ingredient drink.

1½ oz. 12-year Japanese whisky, preferably Hakushu
1 oz. dry vermouth, preferably Dolin
½ oz. pear liqueur
Ice
1 lemon twist, for garnish

In a mixing glass, combine the whisky, vermouth and pear liqueur. Fill the glass with ice, stir well and strain into a chilled coupe. Pinch the lemon twist over the drink and add to the coupe.
—Jason Patz

AULD ALLIANCE

Makes **1** ●●●●●●●●●

For this Scotch cocktail, New York City mixologist Nick Bennett shakes in Calvados and cinnamon syrup to capture the flavors of a baked-apple dessert.

1½ oz. blended Scotch, such as Monkey Shoulder
½ oz. Calvados
¼ oz. Cinnamon Syrup (p. 70)
2 dashes of orange bitters
Ice, plus 1 large cube for serving
1 green apple slice, for garnish

In a mixing glass, combine the Scotch, Calvados, Cinnamon Syrup and bitters. Fill the glass with ice and stir briefly. Strain into a chilled rocks glass over the large ice cube and garnish with the apple slice. —Nick Bennett

● STRONG ● SWEET ● TART ● BITTER ● FRUITY ● HERBAL ● SMOKY ● SPICY

THE CIRCLE OF THE SUN

ACT OF UNION

Makes **1** ⬤⬤○○○○○○○○

After reading And a Bottle of Rum: A History of the New World in Ten Cocktails, *San Diego bartender Meghan Eastman learned that Scotch and rum are often aged in the same barrels. That sparked the idea to combine the two spirits in this tart, refreshing egg white drink.*

1   oz. blended Scotch
1   oz. Jamaican rum, preferably Appleton
¾   oz. Ginger Syrup (p. 82)
¾   oz. fresh lemon juice
1   large egg white
    Ice
    Angostura bitters, for garnish

In a cocktail shaker, combine the Scotch, rum, Ginger Syrup, lemon juice and egg white; shake vigorously. Fill the shaker with ice and shake again. Strain into a chilled rocks glass and dot with a line of the bitters. —*Meghan Eastman*

443 SPECIAL

Makes **1** ⬤○○○○○○○⬤○

The 443 Special has become Nick Bennett's signature cocktail. He created it when he was working at Amor y Amargo in New York. Bennett, now at NYC's Porchlight, says people still ask him to make this smoky Scotch drink laced with honey-sweetened yellow Chartreuse.

1   oz. Highland Scotch, such as Glenmorangie
½   oz. peated Scotch, such as Laphroaig
¾   oz. yellow Chartreuse
¾   oz. Amaro CioCiaro
     Ice
1   lemon twist, for garnish

In a mixing glass, combine both Scotches, the Chartreuse and amaro. Fill the glass with ice, stir well and strain into a chilled coupe. Pinch the lemon twist over the drink and add to the coupe. —*Nick Bennett*

⬤ STRONG ⬤ SWEET ⬤ TART ⬤ BITTER ⬤ FRUITY ⬤ HERBAL ⬤ SMOKY ⬤ SPICY

SHARPIE MUSTACHE

Makes **1** ●○○○●○○○

"Given how strong this cocktail is, it's dangerously drinkable," warns Seattle mixologist Chris Elford. "I first served it to an older woman. I imagined her going back to her senior-citizen sorority house and somebody drawing a Sharpie mustache on her."

¾ oz. rye whiskey
¾ oz. London dry gin
¾ oz. Bonal Gentiane-Quina (slightly bitter French aperitif wine)
¾ oz. Amaro Meletti
  Dash of tiki bitters
  Ice
1 orange twist, for garnish

In a mixing glass, combine the whiskey, gin, Bonal, amaro and bitters. Fill the glass with ice, stir well and strain into a chilled rocks glass. Pinch the orange twist over the drink and add to the glass. —*Chris Elford*

HUMS OF AISLING

Makes **1** ●○○○○○○●○

New York City mixologist Pamela Wiznitzer describes this hot Irish whiskey drink as perfect on a bitter-cold day. According to Wiznitzer, many women in the 1700s and 1800s snuck whiskey into their hot drinks. "Thank goodness there's nothing taboo about a woman enjoying a hot whiskey drink these days," she says.

1 oz. Irish whiskey, preferably Connemara
1 oz. applejack (American apple brandy)
½ oz. Amaro Montenegro
½ oz. Cinnamon Syrup (p. 70)
¼ oz. fresh lemon juice
3 dashes of Angostura bitters
3 dashes of orange bitters
3 oz. hot water
1 star anise pod and a small pinch of freshly grated nutmeg, for garnish

In a warmed mug or heatproof glass, combine the whiskey, applejack, amaro, Cinnamon Syrup, lemon juice, both bitters and hot water. Stir briefly and garnish with the star anise and nutmeg. —*Pamela Wiznitzer*

● STRONG ● SWEET ● TART ● BITTER ● FRUITY ● HERBAL ● SMOKY ● SPICY

FORTITUDE

Makes **1** ●●○○○○○○○○

"Our Founding Fathers were drinking whiskey and rum flips served in taverns," says Pamela Wiznitzer, bartender at Manhattan's Seamstress. For this flip (a sweetened cocktail made with a whole raw egg and spice), she adds sweet sherry, balsamic vinegar and chocolaty mole bitters.

1½ oz. Irish whiskey, preferably Powers John's Lane

¾ oz. banana liqueur, preferably Giffard Banane du Brésil

¾ oz. Pedro Ximénez sherry

¼ oz. St. Elizabeth allspice dram (rum-based allspice liqueur)

1 tsp. balsamic vinegar

3 dashes of Angostura bitters

3 dashes of mole bitters

1 large egg

Ice

Small pinch of freshly grated nutmeg, for garnish

In a cocktail shaker, combine all of the ingredients except the ice and nutmeg; shake vigorously. Fill the shaker with ice and shake again. Strain into a chilled wineglass and garnish with the nutmeg.
—Pamela Wiznitzer

FAIR TRADE

Makes **1** ●○○○○○○○○○

"Cynar and coffee liqueur are great flavor buddies," says Meghan Eastman. Mixed with single-malt Scotch, this pleasantly bitter drink evokes an espresso with a twist of lemon.

2 oz. single-malt Scotch

½ oz. Cynar (bitter artichoke aperitif)

½ oz. coffee liqueur

3 dashes of orange bitters

Ice

1 lemon twist, for garnish

In a mixing glass, combine the Scotch, Cynar, coffee liqueur and bitters. Fill the glass with ice, stir well and strain into a chilled coupe. Pinch the lemon twist over the drink and add to the coupe. —Meghan Eastman

● STRONG ● SWEET ● TART ● BITTER ● FRUITY ● HERBAL ● SMOKY ● SPICY

THE WAY OF THE SWORD

Makes **1** ●●●●●●●●●

*Jason Patz of
Williams & Graham
in Denver riffs on
a Rob Roy with
Japanese whisky (the
classic uses Scotch).
He prefers Yamazaki
12-year, which is
aged in bourbon
casks, sherry casks
and Japanese
oak barrels. While
Japanese whisky
distillers are free
to mix and match
casks, Scotch must be
aged only in oak for
at least three years.*

1½ oz. 12-year Japanese whisky,
    preferably Yamazaki
¾ oz. sweet vermouth, preferably Dolin rouge
½ oz. Cynar (bitter artichoke aperitif)
¼ oz. ruby port, preferably
    Sandeman Founders Reserve
    Ice, plus 1 large cube for serving
1 orange twist

In a mixing glass, combine the whisky, vermouth,
Cynar and port. Fill the glass with ice, stir well
and strain into a chilled double rocks glass over
the large ice cube. Pinch the orange twist
over the drink and discard. —*Jason Patz*

CLASSIC

MINT JULEP

Makes **1** ●●●●●●●●●

*When New Orleans
bartender Chris
McMillian mixes mint
juleps, he recites
an ode written in the
1890s by a Kentucky
newspaperman.
It praises the cocktail
as "the zenith of
man's pleasure...the
very dream of drinks."*

8 mint leaves, plus mint sprigs for garnish
½ oz. Simple Syrup (p. 37)
2 oz. bourbon, preferably overproof
  Crushed ice (p. 27)

In a chilled julep cup or rocks glass, gently muddle
the mint leaves with the Simple Syrup. Add the
bourbon and fill the glass with crushed ice. Spin a
swizzle stick or bar spoon between your hands
to mix the drink. Top with more crushed ice and
garnish with mint sprigs.

● STRONG ● SWEET ● TART ● BITTER ● FRUITY ● HERBAL ● SMOKY ● SPICY

CLASSIC

MANHATTAN

Makes **1**

The Manhattan was one of the first drinks to combine rye with vermouth. Bartenders have since created variations that replace the traditional sweet vermouth, naming the drinks after other areas in New York or other cities.

2 oz. rye whiskey

1 oz. Carpano Antica Formula
  or other sweet vermouth

2 dashes of Angostura bitters
  Ice

1 maraschino cherry, for garnish

In a mixing glass, combine the rye, vermouth and bitters. Fill the glass with ice and stir well. Strain into a chilled coupe and garnish with the cherry.

CLASSIC

SAZERAC

Makes **1**

When it was invented in the 1850s, New Orleans's famous Sazerac cocktail called for Cognac. A decade later, when the phylloxera epidemic in Europe killed off the grapes used to make Cognac, bartenders substituted rye.

¼ oz. absinthe or Pernod

1 sugar cube

3 dashes of Peychaud's bitters

2 dashes of Angostura bitters

2 oz. rye whiskey
  Ice

1 lemon twist

Rinse a chilled rocks glass with the absinthe; pour out the excess. In a mixing glass, muddle the sugar cube with both bitters. Add the rye, fill the glass with ice and stir well to chill the drink and dissolve the sugar. Strain into the prepared rocks glass. Pinch the lemon twist over the drink and discard.

CLASSIC

OLD-FASHIONED

Makes **1** ●○○○○○○○○

According to cocktail historian David Wondrich, the old-fashioned is a direct descendant of the earliest known "true" cocktail, which in 1806 consisted of "a little water, a little sugar, a lot of liquor and a couple splashes of bitters." While it's not traditional, some bartenders muddle a cherry into the drink or add one as garnish.

2 oz. bourbon
¼ oz. Rich Simple Syrup (p. 37)
2 dashes of Angostura bitters
 Ice
1 orange twist and 1 brandied cherry skewered on a pick, for garnish (optional)

In a mixing glass, combine the bourbon, Rich Simple Syrup and bitters. Fill the glass with ice, stir well and strain into an ice-filled rocks glass. Pinch the orange twist over the drink, add it to the glass and garnish with the skewered cherry.

CLASSIC

BLOOD AND SAND

Makes **1** ●●●○○●○○○

This classic's name is a tribute to the 1922 silent movie Blood and Sand, which stars Rudolph Valentino as a poor young Spaniard who eventually becomes a great matador. Fruity and only faintly smoky, it's an approachable drink for people who aren't sure they like Scotch.

 p. 122

1 oz. blended Scotch, such as Compass Box Asyla
1 oz. sweet vermouth
1 oz. cherry liqueur, preferably Heering
1 oz. fresh orange juice
 Ice
1 orange wheel, for garnish

In a cocktail shaker, combine the Scotch, vermouth, cherry liqueur and orange juice. Fill the shaker with ice and shake well. Strain into a chilled martini glass and garnish with the orange wheel.

● STRONG ● SWEET ○ TART ● BITTER ● FRUITY ● HERBAL ● SMOKY ● SPICY

ORCHARD MAI TAI, P. 159

APERITIFS

VODKA

GIN

TEQUILA

RUM

WHISKEY

BRANDY

NIGHTCAPS

BIG BATCH

MOCKTAILS

HOLY ROLLER

Makes **1** ●●●●●●●●○●
Time **10 min**

"Brandy is usually sipped by the fireside, typically by people who have the money to spend on it," says Chris Lowder, bar manager at the NoMad in New York City. He bucks convention, mixing the upscale spirit with Pabst Blue Ribbon and cilantro for a summery, high/ low beer cocktail.

For a mocktail variation, see p. 194.

3	cilantro sprigs
¾	oz. Fennel Syrup (p. 56)
1	oz. unaged grape brandy, such as Rémy Martin V
¾	oz. fresh lime juice
½	oz. Chile Cointreau (below)
	Ice
4	oz. chilled pilsner
1	lime wheel, for garnish

In a cocktail shaker, muddle 2 of the cilantro sprigs with the Fennel Syrup, then add the brandy, lime juice and Chile Cointreau. Fill the shaker with ice and shake well. Fine-strain (p. 27) into a chilled, ice-filled collins glass. Stir in the pilsner and garnish with the lime wheel and remaining cilantro sprig. —*Chris Lowder*

CHILE COINTREAU

In a liquid measuring cup, combine 3 diced unseeded Thai bird chiles with 8½ oz. Cointreau and let stand for 5 minutes. Taste the mixture; when sufficiently spicy, strain the infused Cointreau into a jar and refrigerate for up to 1 month. Makes about 8 oz. —*CL*

●STRONG ●SWEET ●TART ●BITTER ●FRUITY ●HERBAL ●SMOKY ●SPICY

BURNT-SPICE JULEP

Makes **1** ●●●●●●●○○
Time **10 min**

"Customers love this drink like nothing else," says Alba Huerta, owner of Julep in Houston. She flames a tea ball filled with spices and leaves it smoldering in the serving cup, which keeps the aromas in the drink.

2 oz. overproof rum
3 allspice berries, ¼-inch piece of cinnamon stick and 4 cloves, in a small tea ball
12 mint leaves, plus 1 mint sprig for garnish
½ oz. Rich Simple Syrup (p. 37)
1½ oz. bonded apple brandy
½ oz. Jamaican rum, such as Ed Hamilton or Appleton V/X
Dash of Angostura bitters
Crushed ice (p. 27)
1 lemon twist, 3 thin pear or apple slices and a pinch of confectioners' sugar (optional), for garnish

1. In a ramekin, pour the overproof rum over the spice ball.

2. In a chilled julep cup, muddle the mint leaves with the Rich Simple Syrup. Add the apple brandy and Jamaican rum and stir well. Holding the spice ball with tongs, very carefully ignite it with a long match, letting it burn for about 30 seconds. Place the spice ball in the julep cup, then immediately dash the bitters over the spice ball to extinguish the flame. Fill the cup with crushed ice and spin a swizzle stick or bar spoon between your hands to mix the drink. Add more crushed ice and garnish with the mint sprig, lemon twist, fruit slices and confectioners' sugar. Serve with a metal straw.
—*Alba Huerta*

● STRONG ● SWEET ○ TART ● BITTER ● FRUITY ● HERBAL ● SMOKY ● SPICY

AGE D'OR SHIM

Makes **1** ●●●●●●●●○

*Houston bartender
Alba Huerta
combines two grape-
based ingredients:
Cognac and sparkling
red wine. The name
of the drink refers
to the golden age of
cocktails in the South–
the Pierre Ferrand
1840 here is a revival
of the type of Cognac
popular during that
time; a shim is a kind
of low-proof drink.*

One 1-inch piece of lemongrass
(inner bulb only), thinly sliced
¼ oz. Rich Simple Syrup (p. 37)
1 oz. overproof Cognac,
preferably Pierre Ferrand 1840
½ oz. Pineau des Charentes rosé
(Cognac-fortified grape juice)
Crushed ice (p. 27)
2 oz. chilled sparkling red wine
1 bunch of Champagne grapes, for garnish

In a cocktail shaker, gently muddle the lemongrass
with the Rich Simple Syrup, then transfer to a
chilled wineglass. Add the Cognac and Pineau des
Charentes. Fill the glass with crushed ice and spin
a swizzle stick or bar spoon between your hands
to mix the drink. Top with the sparkling wine and
garnish with the grapes. *—Alba Huerta*

IDLE HANDS

Makes **1** ●○○○○○○○○

*New York City
mixologist Chris
Lowder stirs a pinch
of salt into this
Manhattan-style
Cognac cocktail.
"Salt can emphasize
flavors and offset
bitterness," he says.*

1½ oz. overproof Cognac,
preferably Pierre Ferrand 1840
½ oz. Amaro Meletti
½ oz. Carpano Antica Formula
or other sweet vermouth
½ oz. Jamaican rum, such as Appleton V/X
¼ oz. sweet sherry, preferably Pedro Ximénez
Small pinch of salt
Ice
1 grapefruit twist

In a mixing glass, combine the Cognac, amaro,
vermouth, rum, sherry and salt. Fill the glass with
ice, stir well and strain into a chilled coupe. Pinch
the grapefruit twist over the drink and discard.
—Chris Lowder

●STRONG ●SWEET ◐TART ●BITTER ●FRUITY ●HERBAL ●SMOKY ●SPICY

AGE D'OR SHIM

OREGANO COBBLER

Makes **1** ●●●●●●●●●

Alba Huerta, of Julep in Houston, adds fresh oregano to give a savory edge to this cobbler made with pisco, a South American brandy. "Oregano has such a big flavor, you have to tell people up front it's in the cocktail. It can't be a surprise," she says.

3   oregano sprigs
½   oz. Simple Syrup (p. 37)
1½   oz. Italian bianco vermouth, such as Carpano
1   oz. pisco
¼   oz. fino sherry
¼   oz. fresh lemon juice
    Ice cubes, plus cracked ice (p. 27) for serving

In a cocktail shaker, muddle 2 of the oregano sprigs with the Simple Syrup. Add the vermouth, pisco, sherry and lemon juice. Fill the shaker with ice cubes and shake well. Fine-strain (p. 27) into a chilled, cracked-ice-filled highball glass and garnish with the remaining oregano sprig. —*Alba Huerta*

PIQUANT ARMAGNAC SAZERAC

Makes **1** ●●●●●●●●●

Alba Huerta reinvents a Sazerac with spicy ancho chile liqueur and Armagnac—a kind of brandy that was her gateway spirit to mixology. "When I first tried Armagnac, I was like, 'What is this? What's happening here?' It opened up the world of craft cocktails."

⅛   oz. absinthe mixed with ⅛ oz. ancho chile liqueur, in an atomizer
1   oz. Armagnac
1   oz. bonded rye whiskey
¾   tsp. Rich Simple Syrup (p. 37)
4   dashes of Peychaud's bitters
2   dashes of Angostura or Abbott's bitters
    Ice
1   lemon twist and 1 dried ancho chile skewered on a pick, for garnish

Mist a chilled coupe with 3 sprays of the absinthe–ancho chile liqueur mixture. In a mixing glass, combine the Armagnac, whiskey, Rich Simple Syrup and both bitters. Fill the glass with ice and stir well. Strain into the prepared coupe and garnish with the lemon twist and skewered chile. —*Alba Huerta*

● STRONG ● SWEET ● TART ● BITTER ● FRUITY ● HERBAL ● SMOKY ● SPICY

ORCHARD MAI TAI

Makes **1** ●●○●●○●●

"I love mai tais," says Chris Lowder of the NoMad in New York City. "They're so delicious if you make them correctly but terrible if you don't have the right ingredients." He creates this spiced autumnal version with apple brandy and Cognac.

📷 p. 150

For a mocktail variation, see p. 194.

1¼ oz. bonded apple brandy
1 oz. overproof Cognac, preferably Pierre Ferrand 1840
¾ oz. orgeat (almond-flavored syrup)
½ oz. fresh lemon juice
1 tsp. St. Elizabeth allspice dram (rum-based allspice liqueur)
½ tsp. Rich Simple Syrup (p. 37)
½ tsp. fresh ginger juice (from a ½-inch piece of grated ginger pressed through a fine strainer)
Ice cubes, plus crushed ice (p. 27) for serving
3 thin red apple slices, for garnish

In a cocktail shaker, combine all of the ingredients except the ice and garnish. Fill the shaker with ice cubes and shake well. Strain into a chilled, crushed-ice-filled double rocks glass, top with more crushed ice and garnish with the apple slices. —Chris Lowder

BON VIVEUR

Makes **1** ●○○●○●○○●

A bourbon old-fashioned can be harsh and intense, according to Chris Lowder. He swaps in VSOP Cognac and St-Germain for a smoother, lightly floral cocktail.

2 oz. VSOP Cognac
½ oz. St-Germain elderflower liqueur
1 tsp. Bigallet China-China (bitter orange liqueur) or Amaro CioCiaro
Ice, plus 1 large cube for serving
1 grapefruit twist, for garnish

In a mixing glass, combine the Cognac, elderflower liqueur and China-China. Fill the glass with ice, stir well and strain into a double rocks glass over the large ice cube. Pinch the grapefruit twist over the drink and add to the glass. —Chris Lowder

JACK ROSE

Makes **1** ●●○○○○○○○○

One theory suggests this drink was named after (and even invented by) Bald Jack Rose, a notorious New York City hit man in the early 20th century. Another theory says the name refers to the applejack (a type of apple brandy) in the recipe and the rose color created by the grenadine.

 2   **oz. bonded apple brandy**
 ¾   **oz. fresh lemon juice**
 ¾   **oz. grenadine, preferably homemade (p. 37)**
     Ice

In a cocktail shaker, combine the brandy, lemon juice and grenadine. Fill the shaker with ice and shake well. Strain into a chilled coupe.

PISCO SOUR

Makes **1** ●●○○○○○○○○

The pisco sour, a whiskey sour variation, was invented by Victor Morris in Lima, Peru, in the early 1900s. He likely used lime juice, but some pisco sours today use lemon while others use both. Shaking first without ice (a.k.a. dry-shaking) emulsifies the egg white and gives the drink an airy texture.

 2   **oz. pisco**
 ¾   **oz. fresh lime juice**
 ¾   **oz. Simple Syrup (p. 37)**
 1   **large egg white**
     Ice
 4   **drops of Angostura bitters, for garnish**

In a cocktail shaker, combine the pisco, lime juice, Simple Syrup and egg white and shake vigorously. Fill the shaker with ice and shake again. Strain into a chilled coupe. Dot the drink with the bitters and draw a straw through the drops.

●STRONG ●SWEET ○TART ●BITTER ●FRUITY ●HERBAL ●SMOKY ●SPICY

JACK ROSE

SIDECAR

Makes **1**

Legendary mixologist Dale DeGroff explains the name of this classic in The Essential Cocktail: *"If the bartender misses his mark on ingredient quantities so...there's a bit left over in the shaker, he pours that little extra into a shot glass on the side—that little glass is called a sidecar."*

1   orange wedge and sugar
1½   oz. VSOP Cognac
¾   oz. Cointreau
¾   oz. fresh lemon juice
1   orange twist, for garnish
    Ice

Moisten the outer rim of a chilled coupe with the orange wedge and coat lightly with sugar. In a cocktail shaker, combine the Cognac, Cointreau and lemon juice. Fill the shaker with ice, shake well and strain into the prepared coupe. Pinch the orange twist over the drink and add to the coupe.

VIEUX CARRÉ

Makes **1** ●●●●●●●●●

This New Orleans classic, named after the city's French Quarter, was likely created in the 1930s by Walter Bergeron. He tended bar at the establishment that is today called The Carousel Bar.

1   oz. VSOP Cognac
1   oz. rye whiskey
1   oz. sweet vermouth
1   tsp. Bénédictine (spiced herbal liqueur)
    Dash of Peychaud's bitters
    Dash of Angostura bitters
    Ice

In a mixing glass, combine the Cognac, rye, vermouth, Bénédictine and both bitters. Fill the glass with ice, stir well and strain into a chilled, ice-filled rocks glass.

● STRONG   ● SWEET   ● TART   ● BITTER   ● FRUITY   ● HERBAL   ● SMOKY   ● SPICY

BRANDY CRUSTA

Makes **1** ●●○○○○○○○○

This predecessor to the sidecar was invented at the (now defunct) City Exchange bar and café in New Orleans around 1850. NOLA bartender Chris Hannah spikes his modern version with bitters and maraschino liqueur but keeps the sugar rim and signature garnish–a long strip of lemon zest.

1 **lemon wedge and sugar**
1 **long strip of lemon zest**
1½ **oz. VSOP Cognac**
½ **oz. orange curaçao**
½ **oz. fresh lemon juice**
¼ **oz. maraschino liqueur**
2 **dashes of Angostura bitters**
Ice

Moisten the outer rim of a chilled rocks glass with the lemon wedge and coat lightly with sugar. Add the lemon zest to the glass. In a cocktail shaker, combine the Cognac, curaçao, lemon juice, maraschino liqueur and bitters. Fill the shaker with ice and shake well. Strain into the prepared rocks glass.

CORPSE REVIVER NO. 1

Makes **1** ●●○○○○○○○○

Richer and stronger than the more popular gin-based Corpse Reviver No. 2 (p. 85), this classic hair-of-the-dog remedy is designed to bring drinkers back from the dead.

1 **oz. VSOP Cognac**
1 **oz. Calvados**
1 **oz. Carpano Antica Formula or other sweet vermouth**
Ice
1 **maraschino cherry, for garnish**

In a mixing glass, combine the Cognac, Calvados and vermouth. Fill the glass with ice and stir well. Strain into a chilled coupe and garnish with the cherry.

IL SANTO, P. 166

APERITIFS
VODKA
GIN
TEQUILA
RUM
WHISKEY
BRANDY

NIGHTCAPS

BIG BATCH
MOCKTAILS

ROSA AMARGO

Makes **1** ●●●●●●●●●

To give mezcal a pleasant bitterness, Jeremy Oertel, head bartender at Donna in Brooklyn, stirs in grapefruit liqueur. The bracing bitterness of Campari emphasizes the grapefruit flavor.

1½ oz. mezcal
½ oz. Combier Pamplemousse Rose grapefruit liqueur
½ oz. French blanc vermouth, preferably Dolin
½ oz. Campari
  Ice
1 grapefruit twist

In a mixing glass, combine the mezcal, grapefruit liqueur, vermouth and Campari. Fill the glass with ice, stir well and strain into a chilled martini glass or coupe. Pinch the grapefruit twist over the drink and discard. —*Jeremy Oertel*

IL SANTO

Makes **1** ●●●●●●●●●

Karen Grill, general manager of Sassafras Saloon in L.A., was tending bar there when a guest asked her, "What's the point of vermouth?" Her response was this nicely dry nightcap that combines two kinds of vermouth.

📷 p. 164

1 oz. sweet vermouth
1 oz. dry vermouth
2 dashes of orange bitters
  Ice
½ oz. absinthe
1 mint sprig and 1 orange twist, preferably spiral-cut (p. 26), for garnish

In a mixing glass, combine the sweet and dry vermouths with the bitters. Fill the glass with ice and stir well. Strain into a chilled, ice-filled rocks glass and float the absinthe on top, slowly pouring it over the back of a bar spoon near the drink's surface. Garnish with the mint sprig and orange twist. —*Karen Grill*

● STRONG ● SWEET ● TART ● BITTER ● FRUITY ● HERBAL ● SMOKY ● SPICY

ROSA AMARGO

REBEL FLIP

Makes **1** ○●○○○○○○○○

A generous harvest from her neighbor's nut trees led L.A. mixologist Karen Grill to make her own green walnut liqueur. She mixes it into this dessert cocktail that's reminiscent of a boozy milkshake. The drink is equally delicious with nocino, an Italian liqueur made from unripe walnuts.

1 **oz. bourbon**
¾ **oz. heavy cream**
½ **oz. Simple Syrup (p. 37)**
1 **large egg yolk**
½ **oz. walnut liqueur, preferably Nocino della Cristina**
½ **oz. East India sherry**
 Ice
 Pinch of freshly grated nutmeg, for garnish

In a cocktail shaker, combine the bourbon, cream, Simple Syrup, egg yolk, walnut liqueur and sherry and shake vigorously. Fill the shaker with ice and shake again. Strain into a chilled coupe and garnish with the nutmeg. *—Karen Grill*

THE NIGHTCAP

Makes **1** ●○○○○○○○○○

"This is my go-to drink when I'm closing down the bar and doing paperwork at the end of a long shift," says Karen Grill. The simple drink gets extraordinary flavor from Cocchi Vermouth di Torino, a rich, complex alternative to sweet vermouth.

2 **oz. Cocchi Vermouth di Torino or other Italian sweet vermouth**
½ **oz. rye whiskey**
 Dash of orange bitters
 Ice
1 **orange twist, flamed (p. 26), for garnish**

In a chilled rocks glass, combine the vermouth, rye and bitters. Fill the glass with ice and stir well. Flame the twist over the drink and drop it in. *—Karen Grill*

● STRONG ● SWEET ● TART ● BITTER ● FRUITY ● HERBAL ● SMOKY ● SPICY

REBEL FLIP

MAGIC EIGHT BALL

Makes **1** ●●●●●●●●●●

Time **5 min plus infusing the amaro overnight**

Jeremy Oertel makes this nightcap super-chocolaty but not too sweet by steeping cocoa nibs in bittersweet Ramazzotti amaro. "Ramazzotti is cool. It's got these dark Coca-Cola and vanilla flavors in it," he says.

1½ oz. blended Scotch, preferably Monkey Shoulder
¾ oz. Punt e Mes (spicy, orange-accented sweet vermouth)
½ oz. Roasted Cocoa Nib Ramazzotti (below)
1 tsp. single-malt Islay Scotch, such as Laphroaig 10-year
Dash of Angostura bitters
Ice
1 lemon twist, for garnish

In a mixing glass, combine all of the ingredients except the ice and twist. Fill the glass with ice, stir well and strain into a chilled coupe. Pinch the twist over the drink and garnish. —*Jeremy Oertel*

ROASTED COCOA NIB RAMAZZOTTI

In a small skillet, toast 2 Tbsp. cocoa nibs over low heat, stirring, until fragrant, 5 minutes. Transfer to a small bowl with 4 oz. Ramazzotti amaro. Cover and refrigerate overnight. Strain the infused amaro into a jar and refrigerate for up to 1 month. Makes about 4 oz. —*JO*

CHESTER RAPKIN

Makes **1** ●●●●●●●●●●

Brooklyn mixologist Jeremy Oertel created this plummy take on a Negroni for the SoHo Grand Hotel in Manhattan. The name refers to the urban planner who coined the abbreviation "SoHo."

1 oz. sloe gin (liqueur made with gin and sloe berries), preferably Plymouth
1 oz. London dry gin
¾ oz. Campari
¼ oz. St. Elizabeth allspice dram (rum-based allspice liqueur)
Ice
1 orange twist, for garnish

In a mixing glass, combine both gins, the Campari and allspice dram; fill with ice, stir well and strain into a chilled, ice-filled rocks glass. Pinch the twist over the drink and garnish. —*Jeremy Oertel*

● STRONG ● SWEET ● TART ● BITTER ● FRUITY ● HERBAL ● SMOKY ● SPICY

HAUNTED HOUSE

Makes **1** ●●○○○○○○○

Jeremy Oertel spikes this old-fashioned variation with Swedish punsch, a spiced, rum-like liqueur. When he first served the drink at Donna, a Swedish newspaper cited it as an example of the punsch trend in New York City bars.

1 oz. rye whiskey
1 oz. Jamaican rum, preferably Appleton V/X
½ oz. Kronan Swedish punsch
¼ oz. Ginger Syrup (p. 82)
2 dashes of Angostura bitters
  Ice
1 orange twist, for garnish

In a mixing glass, combine the rye, rum, Swedish punsch, Ginger Syrup and bitters. Fill the glass with ice, stir well and strain into a chilled, ice-filled rocks glass. Pinch the orange twist over the drink and add to the glass. —*Jeremy Oertel*

VICE AND VIRTUE

Makes **1** ●●○○○○○●○

Time **15 min**

A Thanksgiving dish of roasted artichokes with brown sugar inspired L.A. bartender Karen Grill to combine artichoke-based Cynar with brown sugar syrup in this simple nightcap.

1½ oz. lightly peated Scotch, such as Glenlivet
¾ oz. Cynar
½ oz. Brown Sugar Syrup (below)
  Ice
1 orange twist, flamed (p. 26), for garnish

In a mixing glass, combine the Scotch, Cynar and Brown Sugar Syrup. Fill the glass with ice, stir well and strain into a chilled coupe. Flame the orange twist over the drink and drop it in. —*Karen Grill*

BROWN SUGAR SYRUP

In a small saucepan, combine 4 oz. water with ½ cup light brown sugar and bring to a boil. Simmer over moderate heat, stirring frequently, until the sugar dissolves, about 3 minutes. Remove from the heat and let cool. Transfer the syrup to a jar and refrigerate for up to 1 month. Makes about 6 oz. —*KG*

● STRONG ● SWEET ○ TART ● BITTER ● FRUITY ● HERBAL ● SMOKY ● SPICY

CLASSIC

WHITE RUSSIAN

Makes **1**

The Dude, played by Jeff Bridges in The Big Lebowski, *fixes his White Russians (or "Caucasians," in Dude-speak) with half-and-half. Lighter versions call for milk, but this recipe goes all the way in the other direction with heavy cream.*

2 oz. vodka
1 oz. coffee liqueur
1 oz. heavy cream
   Ice

In a cocktail shaker, combine the vodka, coffee liqueur and cream. Fill the shaker with ice and shake well. Strain into a chilled, ice-filled rocks glass.

CLASSIC

HOT BUTTERED RUM

Makes **1**

Ghee (clarified butter) mixes with rum more easily than regular butter, giving this hot toddy a silkier texture. Ghee is available in jars at Whole Foods and specialty food markets as well as Indian groceries.

2 oz. dark or amber rum
¾ oz. melted ghee or unsalted butter
   ½ to ¾ oz. honey
4 oz. hot water
   Freshly grated nutmeg, for garnish

In a warmed mug or heatproof glass, combine the rum with the ghee and honey. Stir in the hot water and garnish with the nutmeg.

GRASSHOPPER

Makes **1** ●●●●●●●●●

This shockingly green, creamy cocktail was invented in 1919 but didn't become popular until the Eisenhower era. It's making a comeback today as modern mixologists update the retro classic with ingredients like fresh mint and black pepper.

1 **oz. white crème de cacao**
1 **oz. green crème de menthe**
1 **oz. heavy cream**
　Ice

In a cocktail shaker, combine the crème de cacao, crème de menthe and cream. Fill the shaker with ice and shake well. Strain into a chilled coupe.

IRISH COFFEE

Makes **1** ●●●●●●●●●

San Francisco's Buena Vista restaurant claims to have made America's first Irish coffee, in 1952. One of their patrons, a travel writer named Stanton Delaplane, helped them import the recipe after tasting the drink at Shannon Airport in Ireland.

2 **tsp. light brown sugar**
3 **oz. hot brewed coffee**
1½ **oz. Irish whiskey, preferably Bushmills**
　Dollop of unsweetened whipped cream, for garnish

In a warmed mug or heatproof glass, stir the sugar into the coffee until dissolved. Stir in the whiskey, then garnish with the whipped cream.

● STRONG ● SWEET ● TART ● BITTER ● FRUITY ● HERBAL ● SMOKY ● SPICY

GRASSHOPPER

MADE IN JAPAN, P. 178

APERITIFS
VODKA
GIN
TEQUILA
RUM
WHISKEY
BRANDY
NIGHTCAPS

BIG BATCH

MOCKTAILS

MADE IN JAPAN

Makes **8** ●●●●●●●●

Time **30 min plus steeping and chilling**

Gui Jaroschy, bartender at The Broken Shaker in Miami Beach, gives specific instructions to play the Buck Owens song "Made in Japan" while drinking this sake punch: "Play it on repeat if everyone is so inclined. This is somewhat important," *he deadpans.*

 p. 176

GRAPEFRUIT SYRUP

- **²/₃** cup sugar
- **²/₃** cup water
-   Finely grated zest of ½ grapefruit (about 1 Tbsp.)
- **4** shiso leaves

PUNCH

- **24** oz. junmai sake
- **16** oz. chilled green tea
- **8** oz. St-Germain elderflower liqueur
- **5** oz. Japanese malt whisky, preferably Hakushu 12-year
- **3** oz. fresh lemon juice
- **½** oz. yuzu juice
- **6** dashes of hopped grapefruit bitters
-   Ice
- **24** slices each of apricot and plum, 8 thin slices of ginger and 8 shiso leaves, smacked (p. 27), for garnish

1. Make the grapefruit syrup In a small saucepan, bring the sugar and water to a boil. Simmer over moderate heat, stirring, until the sugar dissolves, 2 to 3 minutes. Let cool, then transfer to a jar, add the grapefruit zest and refrigerate overnight. Transfer the syrup to a blender, add the shiso and puree until smooth, 1 minute. Strain the syrup through cheesecloth into a jar; refrigerate until ready to use, up to 2 weeks.

2. Make the punch In a large pitcher, combine 4 oz. of the grapefruit syrup with the sake, green tea, elderflower liqueur, whisky, lemon juice, yuzu juice and bitters. Refrigerate until chilled, about 2 hours. Fill the pitcher with ice and stir well. Pour the punch into 8 chilled rocks glasses or stemless wineglasses and garnish with the apricot, plum and ginger slices and smacked shiso leaves.
—*Gui Jaroschy*

● STRONG ● SWEET ● TART ● BITTER ● FRUITY ● HERBAL ● SMOKY ● SPICY

THE DE PALMA COCKTAIL

Makes **8** ●●●●●●●●●
Time **10 min plus chilling**

Sean Woods of Deadhorse Hill in Worcester, Massachusetts, pays homage to Brian De Palma, the director of Scarface, with this big-batch cocktail. "It needed a name that was tough and regal," Woods says. Herbal, complex and dry, the De Palma gets its bite from Punt e Mes, the spicy-sweet red vermouth.

8   oz. London dry gin, preferably Citadelle
8   oz. Punt e Mes
4   oz. Amaro Montenegro
2   oz. maraschino liqueur
2   oz. green Chartreuse
    Ice
8   orange twists

In a large pitcher, combine the gin, Punt e Mes, amaro, maraschino liqueur and Chartreuse. Refrigerate until chilled, about 2 hours. Fill the pitcher with ice and stir well. To serve, strain into chilled coupes, then pinch 1 orange twist over each drink and discard. —*Sean Woods*

THE BETTER AVENUE

Makes **8** ●●●●●●●●●
Time **10 min plus chilling**

Beet juice adds tons of earthy flavor to this savory pitcher drink. Sean Woods rims the serving glasses with fresh hops. The version here calls for intensely hoppy beer instead.

10   oz. gin
8   oz. French dry vermouth, preferably Dolin
4   oz. beet juice
4   oz. fresh lemon juice
4   oz. Simple Syrup (p. 37)
2   dashes of celery bitters
    Ice
2   chilled 12-oz. bottles of hoppy beer, such as Dogfish Head 120 Minute IPA

In a large pitcher, combine the gin, vermouth, beet juice, lemon juice, Simple Syrup and bitters. Refrigerate until chilled, about 2 hours. Half-fill the pitcher with ice, add the beer and stir well. Strain into chilled coupes. —*Sean Woods*

MEL'S GIBSON

Makes **8** ●●●●●●●●●

Time **20 min plus 4 days for infusing and chilling**

Nostalgic for "a time when people mixed up martinis in the living room and it was superclassy," Miami Beach bartender Gui Jaroschy was determined to create a drink in an elegant pitcher. The result is this Gibson riff that's extra-savory with pickled onion–infused vermouth and pleasantly herbal with rosemary syrup.

PICKLED-ONION VERMOUTH

9 oz. French dry vermouth, preferably Dolin

8 cocktail onions plus 2 oz. of their pickling liquid

ROSEMARY SYRUP

2 rosemary sprigs

8 oz. Simple Syrup (p. 37)

PUNCH

12 oz. Plymouth gin

20 dashes of lemon bitters, preferably The Bitter Truth

Ice

24 cocktail onions skewered on 8 picks, for garnish

1. Make the pickled-onion vermouth In a jar, combine the vermouth and cocktail onions with their pickling liquid. Refrigerate for 4 days; shake the jar once a day. Pour the infused vermouth through a fine strainer into a jar, pressing down on the onions to extract as much liquid as possible. Reserve the onions for another use.

2. Make the rosemary syrup In a small saucepan, blanch the rosemary in boiling water for 30 seconds. Transfer to ice water to cool. Remove the leaves and transfer to a blender; discard the stems. Add the Simple Syrup and puree until smooth, about 2 minutes. Strain the syrup through cheesecloth into a jar.

3. Make the punch In a large pitcher, combine the gin, 10 oz. of the pickled-onion vermouth, 2 oz. of the rosemary syrup and the lemon bitters; refrigerate until chilled, about 2 hours. Fill the pitcher with ice and stir well. Strain into 8 chilled martini glasses and garnish each drink with the skewered cocktail onions. *—Gui Jaroschy*

● STRONG ● SWEET ○ TART ● BITTER ● FRUITY ◑ HERBAL ● SMOKY ● SPICY

MEL'S GIBSON

THE STRANGE BIRD

Makes **6** ●●●●●●●●●

Time **30 min plus 3 days for clarifying the punch**

"This clarified milk punch is a bit of a bear to produce, but it's worth the work!" promises Chad Arnholt, bartender at The Perennial in San Francisco. While citrus juice is typically added to warm milk to make it curdle, Arnholt uses chopped kiwi, which is also high in acid. He then strains out the curds, leaving behind a wonderfully rich and luscious golden drink.

2 **lbs. kiwi (about 9), peeled and roughly chopped into ½-inch pieces**

1½ **cups cane sugar**

8 **oz. whole milk**

12 **oz. London dry gin**

10 **oz. manzanilla sherry**
Ice cubes, preferably large, for serving
Coffee extract, for garnish

1. In a ½-gallon mason jar or pitcher, combine the kiwi and sugar. Cover and refrigerate for 48 hours.

2. In a medium saucepan, gently simmer the milk over low heat until it develops a thin film and tiny bubbles appear around the edge of the pan, about 10 minutes. Do not let the milk boil.

3. Add the gin and sherry to the kiwi mixture and stir until the sugar is completely dissolved. Pour the warm milk into the kiwi mixture (it will curdle) and let stand for 30 minutes.

4. Strain half of the punch mixture into another jar or pitcher through cheesecloth. Strain the remaining punch through fresh cheesecloth. Cover and refrigerate overnight to allow the remaining curds to settle.

5. Carefully ladle the clear punch into a bottle, without disturbing the solids at the bottom, and refrigerate; discard the curds. The clarified punch can be refrigerated for up to 2 weeks.

6. To serve, pour the punch into chilled rocks glasses over a large ice cube or smaller cubes. Garnish each drink with 1 or 2 drops of coffee extract. —*Chad Arnholt*

● STRONG ● SWEET ● TART ● BITTER ● FRUITY ● HERBAL ● SMOKY ● SPICY

BITCHES' BREW

Makes **8 to 12**

Time **20 min plus chilling**

At The Broken Shaker in Miami Beach, Gui Jaroschy revamps the old-school tiki drink Scorpion Bowl with fresh watermelon juice. He serves the punch in the watermelon rind, allowing guests to drink directly from bendy straws inserted around the rim. "It's the perfect shared cocktail for an intimate group of friends," he says.

1	medium seedless watermelon
20	oz. amber rum
6	oz. Jamaican rum, preferably Smith & Cross
6	oz. coconut rum
12	oz. fresh lime juice
12	oz. Don's Spices #2 (spiced syrup; available from *bgreynolds.com*)
6	oz. Velvet Falernum (clove-spiced liqueur)
10	drops of tiki bitters
	Ice
	Star fruit slices and mint leaves, smacked (p. 27), for garnish
	Cocktail umbrellas and bendy straws, for serving (optional)

1. Using a large knife, slice off the top quarter of the watermelon lengthwise. Using an ice cream scoop, remove the watermelon and reserve, leaving a thin layer of the pink flesh in the watermelon bowl.

2. Juice (or puree in a blender and strain) the reserved watermelon. Add 20 oz. of the watermelon juice to the watermelon bowl (reserve the rest for another use). Add the rums, lime juice, Don's Spices, Velvet Falernum and bitters. Stir well and refrigerate until chilled, about 2 hours.

3. Fill the watermelon bowl with ice, then garnish with the star fruit and smacked mint. To serve, insert cocktail umbrellas into the watermelon rind. Insert straws through the watermelon rim and into the punch and drink directly from the bowl.
—*Gui Jaroschy*

TRAILER PARK SMASH

Makes **20**

Time **15 min plus chilling**

Miami Beach bartender Gui Jaroschy sweetens this rye and beer punch with an easy caraway syrup. For a cheeky garnish, he places two bottles of Miller High Life in the punch bowl for the stragglers who arrive at the end of the night.

CARAWAY SYRUP

8	oz. water
¼	cup caraway seeds
1½	cups sugar

PUNCH

20	oz. overproof rye whiskey
15	oz. fresh lemon juice
10	oz. French rouge vermouth, preferably Dolin
10	oz. chilled unfiltered apple juice
5	oz. cold water
20	dashes of Angostura bitters
	Ice, preferably a 4-inch block, plus ice cubes for serving
2	chilled 12-oz. bottles of pilsner, preferably Miller High Life, plus 2 more clean bottles for garnish
	A large pinch of freshly grated nutmeg and 3 lemon wheels, for garnish (optional)

1. Make the caraway syrup In a small saucepan, combine the water and caraway seeds and bring to a boil. Simmer over low heat for 5 minutes. Stir in the sugar until dissolved. Strain the syrup into a jar and let cool, then refrigerate until ready to use.

2. Make the punch In a punch bowl, combine 8 oz. of the caraway syrup with the whiskey, lemon juice, vermouth, apple juice, water and bitters; stir well. Refrigerate until chilled, about 2 hours. Add the ice, stir in the 2 bottles of beer and garnish with the nutmeg and lemon wheels. Place the remaining 2 bottles of beer in the punch bowl. Ladle the punch into ice-filled plastic cups or collins glasses. —*Gui Jaroschy*

● STRONG ● SWEET ○ TART ● BITTER ● FRUITY ● HERBAL ● SMOKY ● SPICY

TRAILER PARK
SMASH

BELLS OF ST. CLEMENT'S

Makes **8** ●●○○○○○○○

Time **15 min plus 2 days for steeping and chilling**

For this tart, refreshing punch, Sean Woods of Deadhorse Hill in Worcester, Massachusetts, makes his own grenadine and steeps it with hops. "I love the incredibly floral flavor and bitter quality of hops," he says. *Fresh hops are available at home-brew stores and some farmers' markets.*

HOPPED GRENADINE

- 20 oz. grenadine, preferably homemade (p. 37)
- 4 grams fresh hops (about ¼ cup or 11 hops)
  Pinch of salt
- 1 tsp. rose water
- 2 orange twists

PUNCH

- 8½ oz. Aperol
- 8½ oz. rye whiskey, preferably Rittenhouse 100
- 8½ oz. fresh lemon juice
  Ice
- 21 oz. chilled dry sparkling wine

1. Make the hopped grenadine In a saucepan, simmer the grenadine, hops and salt over moderate heat for 8 minutes. Let cool to room temperature, about 1 hour. Transfer to a jar and let steep in the refrigerator for 2 days. Strain into a jar and add the rose water; pinch the orange twists over the hopped grenadine and discard them. Stir, then refrigerate until ready to use.

2. Make the punch In a punch bowl, combine 8½ oz. of the hopped grenadine with the Aperol, rye and lemon juice and stir well. Refrigerate until chilled, about 2 hours. Fill the bowl with ice, stir in the sparkling wine and ladle into chilled, ice-filled rocks glasses. —*Sean Woods*

●STRONG ●SWEET ●TART ●BITTER ●FRUITY ●HERBAL ●SMOKY ●SPICY

THE DICKENS

Makes **4 to 5**

●●●●●●●○

Time **25 min**

Sean Woods created this hot rum punch to salvage a bad batch of drinks. "We hired bartenders to mix up a bunch of things for a staff party," he recalls. "What they made was terrible, but I couldn't just throw it away." He mulls apple cider and three types of rum with cinnamon, then spoons a dollop of absinthe whipped cream onto each serving.

32 oz. unsweetened apple cider
10 oz. spiced rum, preferably Sailor Jerry
 8 oz. white rum, such as Plantation 3 Stars
 4 oz. overproof rum, preferably Smith & Cross
 5 oz. Simple Syrup (p. 37)
½ small cinnamon stick
12 oz. heavy cream
¼ oz. absinthe
 2 Tbsp. sugar
 4 dashes of Angostura bitters

1. In a medium saucepan, warm the apple cider, rums, Simple Syrup and cinnamon stick over moderately low heat for 20 minutes; do not let the rum punch boil.

2. Meanwhile, beat the heavy cream, absinthe, sugar and bitters to firm peaks.

3. Discard the cinnamon stick and ladle the rum punch into warmed mugs or heatproof glasses. Spoon the whipped cream on top. —*Sean Woods*

CLASSIC

PISCO PUNCH

Makes **12** ●●●●●●○○○

Time **10 min plus chilling**

Duncan Nicol, owner of San Francisco's legendary (now defunct) Bank Exchange bar, invented pisco punch in the late 1800s. Pineapple gum syrup, one of the drink's key ingredients, went out of production long ago and became available again only recently; it can be found at smallhandfoods.com.

24 oz. pisco
8 oz. fresh lemon juice (from about 6 lemons)
8 oz. water
One 8½-fl.-oz. bottle pineapple gum syrup
2½ cups fresh pineapple chunks
Ice, preferably 1 large block
Thin pineapple slices, for garnish

In a punch bowl, combine the pisco, lemon juice, water, gum syrup and pineapple chunks. Refrigerate until chilled, about 2 hours. Add ice and stir well. Serve the punch in chilled coupes garnished with pineapple slices.

● STRONG ● SWEET ○ TART ● BITTER ● FRUITY ● HERBAL ● SMOKY ● SPICY

PISCO PUNCH

CLASSIC

RED SANGRIA

Makes **12** ●●●●●●●●●

Time **5 min plus chilling**

Although Spaniards and Portuguese have been drinking sangria for centuries, the brandy-spiked drink didn't make an official appearance in the United States until 1964, at the World's Fair in New York City. This version from master mixologist Bridget Albert also includes brandy, but lower-proof recipes substitute lemon-lime soda.

One 750-ml bottle of fruity red wine, such as Merlot

4 oz. brandy

3 oz. Simple Syrup (p. 37)

1 cup mixed chunks of seeded orange, lemon and lime

Ice

In a large pitcher, combine the wine, brandy, Simple Syrup and fruit. Refrigerate until chilled, about 2 hours. Stir in ice and serve the sangria in chilled wineglasses.

● STRONG ● SWEET ○ TART ● BITTER ● FRUITY ○ HERBAL ● SMOKY ● SPICY

THE SMARTEST
BOY ALIVE, P. 202

APERITIFS
VODKA
GIN
TEQUILA
RUM
WHISKEY
BRANDY
NIGHTCAPS
BIG BATCH

MOCKTAILS

John deBary is the bar director of Momofuku restaurants and chief mixologist for F&W Cocktails. Besides curating and testing the drinks in this book, he developed the mocktails, all ingenious versions of cocktails from this edition.

HOLIEST ROLLER

Makes 1 ●●●●●●●○●

"*When I come up with mocktails, the challenge is to keep the flavors 'adult' and spirit-like,*" *says deBary. For this revamp of the brandy-based Holy Roller (p. 152), he amps up nonalcoholic beer with assertive ingredients like cilantro, jalapeño and lime.*

3 cilantro sprigs, plus 1 cilantro leaf, smacked (p. 27), for garnish
3 seeded jalapeño slices
¾ oz. fresh lime juice
¾ oz. Fennel Syrup (p. 56)
Ice
4 oz. nonalcoholic beer, such as O'Doul's
1 lime wheel, for garnish

In a cocktail shaker, muddle the cilantro sprigs with the jalapeño, then add the lime juice and Fennel Syrup. Fill the shaker with ice and shake well. Fine-strain (p. 27) into a chilled, ice-filled collins glass, stir in the beer and garnish with the lime wheel and smacked cilantro leaf.

MORNING MAI TAI

Makes 1 ●○●●●○●●●

Apple cider stands in here for the apple brandy in the Orchard Mai Tai (p. 159). "The ginger syrup and spiced cider re-create the 'heat' that you experience when drinking spirits," *deBary says.*

1½ oz. chilled apple cider, preferably spiced
½ oz. apple cider vinegar
½ oz. Ginger Syrup (p. 82)
½ oz. fresh lemon juice
½ oz. orgeat (almond-flavored syrup)
Ice cubes, plus crushed ice (p. 27) for serving
4 thin red apple slices, for garnish

In a cocktail shaker, combine the apple cider, apple cider vinegar, Ginger Syrup, lemon juice and orgeat. Fill the shaker with ice cubes and shake well. Strain into a chilled, crushed-ice-filled double rocks glass, add more crushed ice and arrange the apple slices in a fan on top.

● STRONG ● SWEET ○ TART ● BITTER ● FRUITY ● HERBAL ○ SMOKY ● SPICY

MORNING MAI TAI

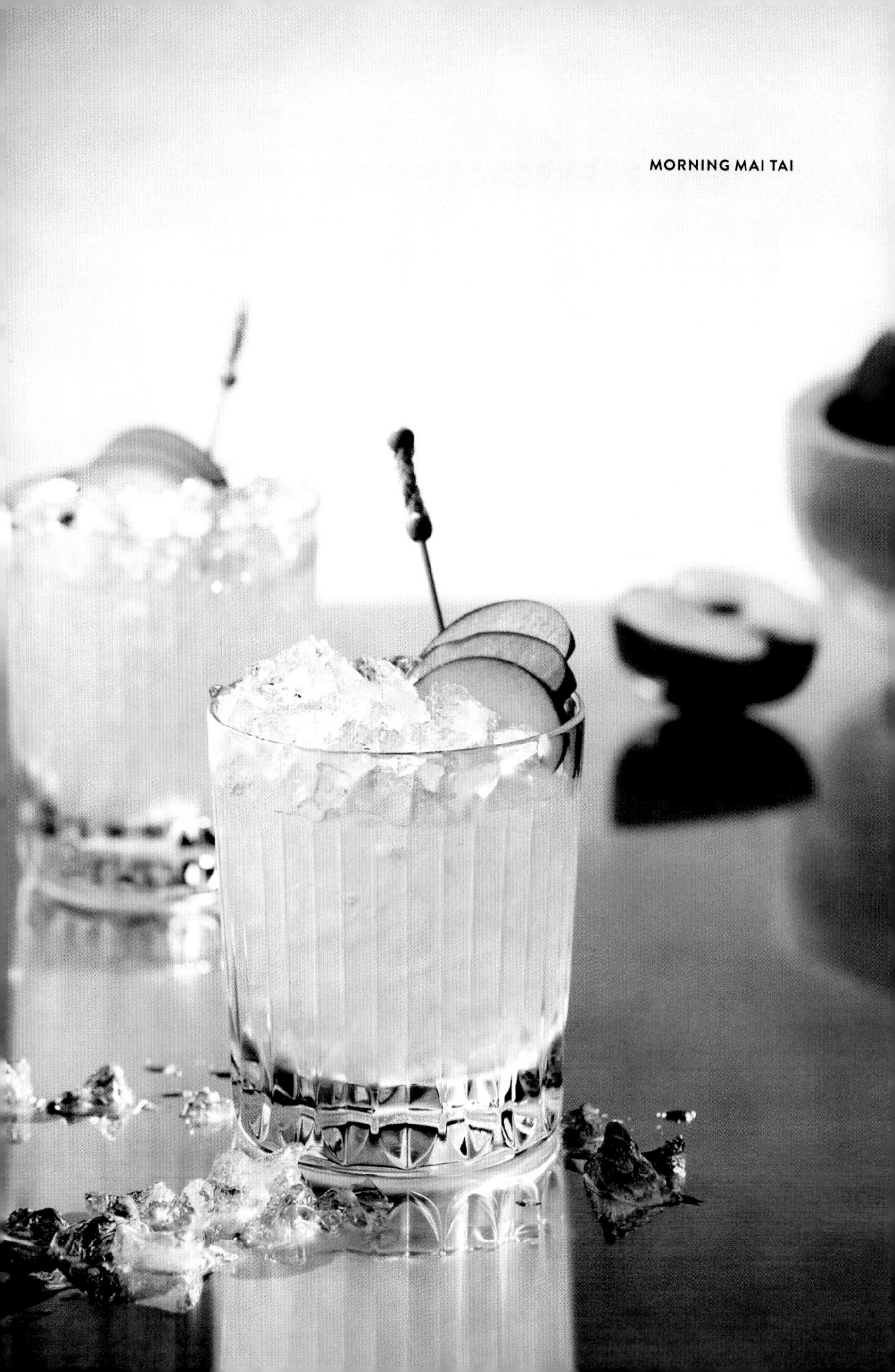

CHARLESTON SHRUB

Makes **1** ●●○○○○○○○○

In this supertangy mocktail, John deBary combines two new additions to the mocktail arsenal: verjus (unripe grape juice) and DIY vinegar. The pineapple vinegar is from Ryan Casey, whose Charleston Sour (p. 124) inspired this recipe.

1½ oz. Pineapple Vinegar (p. 124)
1 oz. chilled verjus (see Note)
¾ oz. Honey Syrup (p. 37)
½ oz. fresh lemon juice
    Ice
2 oz. chilled club soda

In a cocktail shaker, combine the Pineapple Vinegar, verjus, Honey Syrup and lemon juice. Fill the shaker with ice and shake well. Strain into a chilled, ice-filled highball glass and stir in the club soda.

Note Verjus, the tart juice pressed from unripe grapes, is available at specialty food stores.

THE BIRDS AND THE BEES

Makes **1** ●●●●●○●○○
Time **5 min plus steeping the syrup**

"When I'm making mocktails, flavored syrups are my best friend," deBary says. He sweetens this ultra-refreshing, virgin take on The Birds and the Blossoms (made with lemon verbena–infused vodka, p. 58) with a quick lemon verbena syrup. It has a lovely citrus-floral flavor that's also fabulous in iced tea.

1½ oz. Lemon Verbena Syrup (below)
1 oz. fresh lemon juice
½ oz. Honey Syrup (p. 37)
    Ice
4 oz. chilled tonic water
1 lemon balm sprig, for garnish (optional)

In a chilled collins glass, combine the Lemon Verbena Syrup, lemon juice and Honey Syrup. Fill the glass with ice and stir well. Stir in the tonic water and garnish with the lemon balm.

LEMON VERBENA SYRUP
In a small saucepan, boil 8 oz. water. Remove from the heat and add ¼ cup dried lemon verbena leaves. Cover and let steep for 5 minutes. Strain; discard the lemon verbena. Stir in ½ cup sugar until dissolved. Let cool, transfer to a jar and refrigerate for up to 3 weeks. Makes about 10 oz.

● STRONG ● SWEET ○ TART ○ BITTER ● FRUITY ● HERBAL ● SMOKY ● SPICY

DEEPEST PURPLE, REPRISE

Makes **1**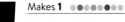

Based on the Deep Purple, Reprise aperitif (p. 48), this mocktail tastes like a sophisticated grape soda. The Japanese herb shiso adds a hit of floral flavor.

6 **Concord grapes**
3 **shiso leaves**
½ **oz. Simple Syrup (p. 37)**
3 **oz. chilled verjus (see Note on p. 196)**
3 **ice cubes, plus crushed ice (p. 27) for serving**
2 **oz. chilled club soda**

In a cocktail shaker, muddle the grapes and 2 of the shiso leaves with the Simple Syrup. Add the verjus and ice cubes and shake well. Fine-strain (p. 27) into a chilled, crushed-ice-filled rocks glass. Stir in the club soda and garnish with the remaining shiso leaf.

BABY MARMALADE

Makes **1** ●●●●●●●●●

John deBary uses both ginger juice and ginger syrup in this mocktail rendition of Lady Marmalade (p. 60). "Ginger replicates that pleasant burn from the vodka in the original," he says.

1 **oz. chilled verjus (see Note on p. 196)**
1 **oz. Ginger Syrup (p. 82)**
¾ **oz. fresh ginger juice (from a 2-inch piece of grated ginger pressed through a fine strainer)**
¾ **oz. grenadine, preferably homemade (p. 37)**
Ice
1½ **oz. chilled club soda**

In a mixing glass, combine the verjus, Ginger Syrup, ginger juice and grenadine. Fill the glass with ice and stir well. Strain into a chilled coupe and stir in the club soda.

●STRONG ●SWEET ○TART ●BITTER ●FRUITY ●HERBAL ●SMOKY ●SPICY

BABY MARMALADE

THE THISTLE IN THE PECK

Makes **1** ⬤⬤⬤⬤⬤⬤⬤⬤⬤

This sweet-tart mocktail is based on Jacyara de Oliveira's vodka cocktail The Thistle in the Kiss (p. 56). Both versions use a delightfully herbal fennel syrup.

3	basil leaves, plus 1 basil sprig for garnish
1½	oz. Fennel Syrup (p. 56)
1¾	oz. fresh lime juice
	Ice, plus 1 large cube for serving

In a cocktail shaker, muddle the 3 basil leaves with the Fennel Syrup. Add the lime juice, then fill the shaker with ice and shake well. Fine-strain (p. 27) into a chilled rocks glass over the large ice cube and garnish with the basil sprig.

PSYCHEDELIC BACKYARD

Makes **1** ⬤⬤⬤⬤⬤⬤⬤⬤⬤

To re-create the flavor of the banana liqueur in the Psychedelic Jungle rum cocktail (p. 110), John deBary shakes a chunk of banana into this mocktail version. He rims just half the glass with salt so you can choose when to take salty sips.

1	lime wedge and coarse salt
1	thin seeded jalapeño slice
	One 1-inch-thick banana slice
1½	oz. chilled verjus (see Note on p. 196)
1	oz. Raspberry Syrup (p. 78)
¾	oz. fresh lime juice
	Ice

Moisten half of the outer rim of a chilled coupe with the lime wedge and coat lightly with salt. In a cocktail shaker, muddle the jalapeño. Add the banana, verjus, Raspberry Syrup and lime juice. Fill the shaker with ice, shake well and fine-strain (p. 27) into the prepared coupe.

⬤ STRONG ⬤ SWEET ⬤ TART ⬤ BITTER ⬤ FRUITY ⬤ HERBAL ⬤ SMOKY ⬤ SPICY

PSYCHEDELIC
BACKYARD

ELI CASH'S BABY

<u>Makes **1**</u> ●●●●●●●○●

John deBary loves Fentimans offbeat dandelion and burdock root soda both on its own and mixed into drinks. "It has an intriguing herbal bitterness that you find in many Italian liqueurs," he says. He uses the soda in place of the amaro in the bourbon-based Eli Cash (p. 132).

2½ oz. chilled Fentimans dandelion and burdock root soda (available from *amazon.com*)
2½ oz. chilled root beer
½ oz. Ginger Syrup (p. 82)
  Ice
1 orange twist, for garnish

In a mixing glass, combine both sodas with the Ginger Syrup. Fill the glass with ice, stir well and strain into a chilled coupe. Pinch the orange twist over the drink and add to the coupe.

THE SMARTEST BOY ALIVE

<u>Makes **1**</u> ●●●●●●●○○

This hot toddy is a virgin take on The Smartest Man Alive (p. 130). It gets depth of flavor from black tea and delicious complexity from Fentimans dandelion and burdock root soda.

📷 p. 192

2 oz. Fentimans dandelion and burdock root soda (available from *amazon.com*)
1 oz. fresh lemon juice
½ oz. Honey Syrup (p. 37)
5 oz. hot brewed black tea
1 lemon wheel, for garnish

In a small saucepan, heat the soda, lemon juice and Honey Syrup over moderate heat until the mixture is hot and the soda is flat, 2 to 3 minutes. Stir in the tea. Pour into a warmed mug or heatproof glass and garnish with the lemon wheel.

●STRONG ●SWEET ○TART ●BITTER ●FRUITY ●HERBAL ●SMOKY ●SPICY

THE MISADVENTURES OF PETE AND PEACH

Makes 1 ●●●●●●○○

To create a big, billowy foam head, deBary shakes an egg white into this mocktail variation on The Adventures of Pete and Peach (p. 134). Smoky Lapsang souchong tea mimics the peatiness of the Scotch in the original.

2 oz. chilled strong-brewed Lapsang souchong tea
1 oz. chilled peach nectar
¾ oz. Simple Syrup (p. 37)
½ oz. fresh lemon juice
1 large egg white
Ice
1 peach slice, for garnish

In a cocktail shaker, combine the tea, peach nectar, Simple Syrup, lemon juice and egg white; shake vigorously. Fill the shaker with ice and shake again. Strain into a large chilled coupe and garnish with the peach slice.

MAGNETIC ROLE REVERSAL

Makes 1 ●●●●●●○○

The basil-cucumber puree here is from Jay Schroeder, whose Magnetic Pole Reversal tequila cocktail (p. 92) inspired this mocktail. For a drier version, stir in tonic water; for a sweeter drink, use lemon-lime soda instead.

2 oz. Basil-Cucumber Puree (p. 92)
1 oz. fresh lime juice
Pinch of salt
Ice
4 to 4½ oz. chilled tonic water, preferably Fever-Tree Indian, or lemon-lime soda
3 basil leaves, smacked (p. 27), for garnish

In a cocktail shaker, combine the Basil-Cucumber Puree, lime juice and salt. Fill the shaker with ice and shake well. Strain into a chilled, ice-filled double rocks glass and stir in the tonic water. Clap the basil leaves between your hands over the drink to release the essential oils and add them to the glass.

KYLE LINDEN WEBSTER
AT EXPATRIATE
IN PORTLAND,
OREGON, P. 216

TOP
100
NEW
BARS

Food & Wine editors compiled this definitive list of the country's best new bars and lounges, several of them led by the rising star mixologists in this book. These destinations have outstanding drinks in every conceivable form—from cocktails on tap at a former soda fountain in San Diego (Polite Provisions, p. 215) to a menu that includes vaporized, inhalable cocktails at a hyper-experimental restaurant in Boston (Café ArtScience, p. 206).

East Coast

BOSTON AREA

Café ArtScience

At this molecular-minded restaurant and bar, Todd Maul creates flavor-altering ice cubes—the ones with candied violets transform a gin-cucumber collins as they melt—and vaporizes inhalable drinks. *650 E. Kendall St., Cambridge; 857-999-2193; cafeartscience.com.*

Carrie Nation

Carrie Nation was the woman known for vandalizing bars during the temperance movement of the early 1900s. The main bar and upstairs speakeasy here serve a variety of whiskeys and cocktails with names like December 5th—the date Prohibition was repealed. *11 Beacon St., Boston; 617-227-3100; carrienationcocktailclub.com.*

Highball Lounge

This casual lounge in the Nine Zero Hotel appeals to a nostalgia for childhood with board games and a menu that you read through a 3-D View-Master. Creative drinks include the Wallflower, a mix of gin, orange vermouth, basil and honey-lavender essence. *90 Tremont St., Boston; 617-772-0202; highballboston.com.*

State Park

At this supercasual dive bar decorated with taxidermied animals and neon beer signs, guests sip cocktails like the caramelized rye Green Walnut and share pitchers of Jack & Maine Coke while playing pool, shuffleboard and pinball. *1 Kendall Sq., Building 300, Cambridge; 617-848-4355; statepark.is.*

Tavern Road

Located in the up-and-coming Fort Point neighborhood, Tavern Road specializes in seasonal handcrafted drinks like Fishnets and Fangs (mezcal, Peychaud's bitters and Drambuie). Notable on the menu: a rotating list of cocktail flights. *343 Congress St., Boston; 617-790-0808; tavernroad.com.*

PORTLAND, MAINE

Portland Hunt & Alpine Club

In a city that's only starting to explore mixology, PHAC stands out for its original craft cocktails. One to try: White Noise, made with Cocchi Americano, elderflower liqueur and grapefruit zest. It's delicious paired with dishes from the Scandinavian-themed menu. *75 Market St.; 207-747-4754; huntandalpineclub.com.*

NEW YORK CITY

Attaboy

This speakeasy in the former Milk & Honey space is run by two M&H vets, Sam Ross and Michael McIlroy. Guests order drinks based on spirit and flavor preference rather than from a printed menu. The check arrives in one of the out-of-print books from the shelves. *134 Eldridge St., Manhattan; no phone; no website.*

Bar Sardine

This compact neighborhood bar in the West Village serves inspired drinks from Brian Bartels, like Dance Up That Alley (two kinds of gin, coconut water and cucumber), alongside barrel-aged selections. *183 W. 10th St., Manhattan; 646-360-3705; barsardinenyc.com.*

Boilermaker

Beer-and-shot pairings are the house specialty, though the intimate bar also makes fine, well-priced craft cocktails like the creamy La Piña Verde (green Chartreuse, lime, pineapple juice and coconut cream). *13 First Ave., Manhattan; 212-995-5400; boilermakernyc.com.*

The Dead Rabbit
This Financial District saloon from onetime UK-based bartenders Sean Muldoon and Jack McGarry is a nod to old New York. The taproom offers whiskeys and beer; the upstairs parlor serves more than 70 historically accurate classic cocktails. *30 Water St., Manhattan; 646-422-7906; deadrabbitnyc.com.*

Donna
Jeremy Oertel (p. 33) categorizes drinks at this late-night Williamsburg lounge by style and flavor (light-bodied and approachable to full-bodied and adventurous). Drinks like the Caribbean-inspired punches on draft or the cachaça-based Downward Spiral are great with bar bites from the Brooklyn Taco Co. pop-up. *27 Broadway, Brooklyn; 646-568-6622; donnabklyn.com.*

The Happiest Hour
At this retro-tropical bar lined with palm tree wallpaper and sunglass-wearing alligator heads, guests select the base spirit for Karen Fu (p. 31) to mix into their drink. Choose jalapeño tequila, rum or gin for the Link Ray; gin, rum or pisco for the Loose Lemon. *121 W. 10th St., Manhattan; 212-243-2827; happiesthournyc.com.*

The Long Island Bar
Toby Cecchini lovingly restored an old diner to create this retro bar and restaurant. Try one of his revamped classics, like the Long Island Gimlet (with ginger-lime cordial), along with the chef's specialty: butterscotch pudding. *110 Atlantic Ave., Brooklyn; 718-625-8908; thelongislandbar.com.*

The NoMad Bar
At its new location, this bi-level bar evokes glamorous Old New York. Bar director Leo Robitschek and bar manager Chris Lowder (p. 33) offer classics like the Pimm's Cup as well as reserve cocktails priced between $28 and $198 (the Vieux Carré, made with 50-year-old Cognac and specialty rye whiskey). *1170 Broadway, Manhattan; 212-796-1500; thenomadhotel.com.*

Roof at Park South
This elegant bar on top of the Park South Hotel has unobstructed views of New York City's skyline. Bar director Ted Kilpatrick mixes unique cocktails like Baby in a Corner: 10-year-old Scotch, elderflower liqueur and the Hungarian herb liqueur Zwack. *125 E. 27th St., Manhattan; 212-204-5222; roofatparksouth.com.*

PHILADELPHIA

1 Tippling Place
The menu at this cozy, parlor-like venue has seasonal punches and barrel-aged classic cocktails like the Mexican Strawberry, made with tequila, cucumber and mint. The signature drink: Fish House Punch, with rum and brandy. *2006 Chestnut St.; 215-665-0456; 1tpl.com.*

Charlie Was a Sinner
The plant-based (a.k.a. vegan) menu means that cocktails are largely fruit-, vegetable- and herb-based, sweetened with honey alternatives and sometimes infused with farro or tobacco. The Beetlejuice, for example, is made with applejack, Prosecco, beets, blueberries, lemon and Demerara sugar. *131 S. 13th St.; 267-758-5372; charliewasasinner.com.*

WASHINGTON, DC

2 Birds, 1 Stone
This bright and lively cocktail bar is the newest outpost from the team behind Proof and Estadio. Adam Bernbach serves original drinks like the Darkside, made with gin, Barolo Chinato and star anise, and the whiskey-and-Chartreuse-based Our Lady of the Harbor. *1800 14th St. NW; no phone; 2birds1stonedc.com.*

Dram & Grain

This reservations-only, speakeasy-style bar has three seatings a night. The 15-cocktail menu rotates every month; past offerings include the Brooklyn, mixed with the bartender's own house-made version of the French liqueur Amer Picon. *2007 18th St. NW; 202-607-1572; facebook .com/DramandGrain.*

The Partisan

The bar at this meat-centric restaurant features novel cocktails by Jeff Faile. Today Your Love, one favorite, is made with Ransom Old Tom gin, fortified wine and the herbaceous liqueur Kina L'Avion d'Or. There are also 25 wines and spirits on tap plus funky sour beers to drink with one of the impressive charcuterie plates. *709 D St. NW; 202-524-5322; thepartisandc.com.*

Red Light

This casual dessert and cocktail bar with an elegant streetside patio specializes in boozy sweets and original drinks. One to try: the Riverstone Slush, made with ice wine, Aperol, fruit nectar and winter fruit. *1401 R St. NW; 202-234-0400; redlightbardc.com.*

Rose's Luxury

There's invariably a wait for the upstairs cocktail bar at this charming restaurant. Rose's short list of impeccable drinks includes the Americano, made with amaro, Aperol and grapefruit, and a Thai basil-infused tequila and ginger beer cocktail. *717 Eighth St. SE; 202-580-8889; rosesluxury.com.*

Southern Efficiency

Bar manager J.P. Fetherston creates a full gamut of drinks with whiskey and other ingredients sourced from traditional and craft distillers. The soda for the White Whiskey and Smoked Cola cocktail is made and smoked in house. *1841 Seventh St. NW; 202-316-9396; whiskeyhome.com.*

Midwest

DETROIT

Wright & Co.

The centerpiece of this restaurant, built in a ballroom-turned-jewelry shop, is the endless white marble bar top. Craft cocktails include the tequila-based El Pajaro Diablo, made with Chartreuse and yellow watermelon juice. *1500 Woodward Ave., Second Floor; 313-962-7711; wrightdetroit.com.*

CHICAGO

Analogue

At this intimate Logan Square bar, Robby Haynes and Henry Prendergast serve Cajun-style dishes alongside a rotating list of cocktails like the Old Fashioned Shot: bourbon laced with sugar and garnished with a bitters-soaked orange wedge. *2523 N. Milwaukee Ave.; 773-904-8567; analoguechicago.com.*

The Berkshire Room

Guests who order dealer's-choice cocktails select a spirit, flavor profile and glass and are rewarded with a drink custom-made by Benjamin Schiller. There's also a concise menu with offerings like the Weston: wheated bourbon mixed with Dark Matter Coffee essence and pipe tobacco. *15 E. Ohio St.; 312-894-0945; theberkshireroom.com.*

Billy Sunday

At this gourmet gastropub, guests enjoy exquisitely crafted drinks like Handle w/Care: tequila, falernum and bitters made from tonka beans—vanilla-scented beans from South and Central America. *3143 W. Logan Blvd.; 773-661-2485; billy-sunday.com.*

SOUTHERN EFFICIENCY
WASHINGTON, DC

Bordel
Red velvet curtains and
risqué wall sketches give
this lounge and cabaret
a sexy, Moulin Rouge vibe.
Drinks from Alex Renshaw
(p. 35) and his fellow bartenders are likewise seduc-
tive: The menu includes
tea party–style punches,
classics and house cock-
tails like pisco-honey Babe
in the Woods. *1721 W.
Division St.; 773-227-8600;
bordelchicago.com.*

Celeste
Celeste pays homage to
the spirit of innovation
celebrated by the 1893
Chicago World's Fair.
Drinks rooted in science
(such as The Prelude, a
bottled cocktail made with
orange oil) are served
in a modern and refined
barroom. *111 W. Hubbard St.;
312-828-9000;
celestechicago.com.*

Sportsman's Club
In a softly lit space with
checkerboards built into
the tables, Jacyara de
Oliveira (p. 29) uses a few
simple ingredients to
make stellar drinks, which
change daily. The one
constant is the Sportsman's
Club Cocktail, made with
bourbon, Zucca rhubarb
amaro and Luxardo bitters.
*948 N. Western Ave.;
872-206-8054;
drinkingandgathering.com.*

Three Dots and a Dash
This tiki-style bar is named
for a 1940s cocktail made
with two types of rum,
falernum and honey; three
dots and a dash is also
Morse code for V, as in
victory. Its Western-style
sister establishment,
Bub City, is upstairs.
*435 N. Clark St.; 312-610-
4220; threedotschicago.com.*

INDIANAPOLIS

Libertine Liquor Bar
The drinks at this recently
relocated downstairs
space range from classics
to more original concoc-
tions such as the gin-and-
neroli-inflected Screw &
Bolt. The menu names
each recipe's creator or
historical origin.
*608 Massachusetts Ave.; 317-
631-3333; libertineindy.com.*

Thunderbird
Cocktails at Thunderbird's
U-shaped bar are divided
into three categories:
Old Standards, like the
Sazerac and Negroni;
Over-Hyped, including the
Blanche Devereaux, made
with rye, apricot liqueur,
grapefruit and honey; and
For the Tiki Gods, such as
the rum-and-coconut-
cream-based Gorilla Grog.
*1127 Shelby St.; 317-974-
9580; thunderbirdindy.com.*

MILWAUKEE

Goodkind
Bartender Katherine Rose
collaborates with Good-
kind's chefs to design
perfect food-and-cocktail
pairings. One to try: spicy
crab bucatini with the
Tiger House (reposado
tequila, Suze, lime and
house-made sweet pepper
agave syrup). *2457 S. Went-
worth Ave.; 414-763-4706;
goodkindbayview.com.*

Lucky Joe's Tiki Room
This tropical-themed bar and lounge is decorated with giant hand-carved tiki sculptures and puffer fish–shaped lights hanging from the bamboo ceiling. Drinks are wacky but delicious riffs on classic tiki cocktails, such as a peach pie–flavored mai tai. *196 S. Second St.; 414-271-8454; luckyjoestiki.com.*

MADISON, WISCONSIN

Forequarter
This rustic restaurant organizes its drinks list into sections like Refreshing (including the Wiscosmopolitan, made with milk vodka, curaçao and lime), Tart (the tequila-based La Taqueria) and Light/Fizzy (Elderflower 75). *708¼ E. Johnson St.; 608-609-4717; forequartermadison.com.*

Heritage Tavern
Grant Hurless works with local growers to source ingredients for his seasonally changing cocktail menu. For example, he finds fresh lavender to mix into his vodka-based Fox Trot. *131 E. Mifflin St.; 608-283-9500; heritagetavern.com.*

MATEO BAR DE TAPAS
DURHAM, NC

MINNEAPOLIS

Coup d'Etat
This vast, 9,000-square-foot restaurant and bar consists of several dining rooms and upper- and lower-level patios. The cocktail menu features new creations as well as reinvented classics like the Manhattan-martini hybrid A Lifetime of Todays. *2923 Girard Ave. S.; 612-354-3575; coupdetatmpls.com.*

Parlour
Barman Jesse Held uses fresh juices, house-made syrups and rare, artisanal spirits to create cocktails based on traditional favorites. He mixes his Spicy n' Stormy with house-spiced black rum. *730 N. Washington Ave.; 612-354-3135; boroughmpls.com.*

ST. LOUIS

Planter's House
This restaurant is named for a hotel that was a St. Louis landmark for more than 100 years. Classic cocktails include sours, collinses, fizzes, slings and large-format, bottled Negronis and Sazeracs. *1000 Mississippi Ave.; 314-696-2603; plantershousestl.com.*

KANSAS CITY, MISSOURI

The Kill Devil Club
Bartender-restaurateur Ryan Maybee consulted on the opening of this "adult oasis" that specializes in live jazz. The punches serve six to eight and range from the spiced Kill Devil Punch to the "complex, interesting and adventurous" pisco punch. *31 E. 14 St.; 816-674-4137; killdevilclub.com.*

WICHITA, KANSAS

Monarch
In the historic Delano District, this gastropub, café and lounge has a menu dedicated entirely to whiskey, with an emphasis on bourbon—also featured in cocktails like The Perfect Manhattan and the Apple Bourbon Sour. *579 W. Douglas; 316-201-6626; monarchwichita.com.*

South

LOUISVILLE, KENTUCKY

Down One Bourbon Bar
Located on what locals call Whiskey Row, this casual spot has a collection of 120 bourbons, including rare bottles. Try a bourbon flight or order a bourbon cocktail like the 7 Across the Board, with blackberries and raspberry-sage syrup. *321 W. Main St.; 502-566-3259; downonebourbonbar.com.*

El Camino
This surf-punk-meets-Mexican-street-food-cart-and-tiki-bar serves tropical drinks like mai tais and punch bowls. Their Luau Scorpion is a throwback to a classic 1950s recipe. *1314 Bardstown Rd.; 502-454-5417; elfreakingcamino.com.*

NASHVILLE

The 404 Kitchen
Part of the boutique 404 Hotel, this small, ingredient-driven restaurant is housed in a repurposed shipping container. Drinks are unconventional: The Nearest Green is made with Tennessee whiskey, apple brandy, Benton's bacon and citrus-infused honey. *404 12th Ave. S.; 615-251-1404; the404nashville.com.*

Husk
Husk's rotating menu of classic cocktails honors Nashville history and chef Sean Brock's commitment to local, seasonal ingredients. One recent offering: Belle of Georgia, with Weller 107 bourbon, house-smoked bourbon pecan cordial, peach and tobacco bitters. *37 Rutledge St.; 615-256-6565; husknashville.com.*

Pinewood Social
With a bowling alley, a bocce court and two (small) swimming pools, Pinewood Social encourages lingering. Drinks from bar manager Matt Tocco range from original cocktails like the rye-absinthe District 9 to pitchers of the house-made shandy. *33 Peabody St.; 615-751-8111; pinewoodsocial.com.*

RICHMOND, VIRGINIA

Dutch and Company
A wide assortment of spirits and innovative cocktails highlight Michelle Peake-Shriver's drinks list. She mixes her Basil Smash with vodka, elderflower liqueur, grapefruit cordial and lemon. *400 N. 27th St.; 804-643-8824; dutchand company.tumblr.com.*

NORTH CAROLINA

The Imperial Life
This low-lit, intimate bar and lounge features an extensive spirits selection, esoteric wine varietals, local beers and classic and barrel-aged cocktails. The bartender's choice is a good default for indecisive drinkers. *48 College St., Asheville; 828-254-9980; imperialbarasheville.com.*

Mateo Bar de Tapas
Guests can take advantage of the impressive sherry collection—one of the largest in the country—by ordering a glass, a bottle or a tasting flight. Or sample a house cocktail, perhaps the Rye Malvado, made with amontillado sherry, vermouth and saffron. *109 W. Chapel Hill St., Durham; 919-530-8700; mateotapas.com.*

CHARLESTON, SOUTH CAROLINA

Edmund's Oast

Named for "The Rebel Brewer," an Englishman known for donating money to the American Revolution, Edmund's Oast serves over 75 beers as well as inventive cocktails made by Ryan Casey (p. 29). His creations include single servings of the Chatham Artillery Punch on draft and the mezcal-and-tequila-based It Takes a Village Idiot. *1081 Morrison Dr.; 843-727-1145; edmundsoast.com.*

Minero

The decidedly Mexican-inspired cocktail menu has the requisite margarita and sangria, but also less expected creations like El Satánico: tequila, Chartreuse, pineapple vinegar and tepache (a fermented pineapple liqueur). All drinks pair well with the restaurant's stellar tacos. *155 E. Bay St.; 843-789-2241; minerorestaurant.com.*

The Ordinary

The drinks menu at chef Mike Lata's oyster bar is tightly focused, offering just a handful of carefully crafted cocktails at a time. A recent concoction: the Echo, Echo, made with gin, grapefruit, green Chartreuse and falernum. *544 King St.; 843-414-7060; eattheordinary.com.*

ATLANTA AREA

Kimball House

In an 1891 railway depot, Kimball House specializes in oysters, absinthe service and Miles Macquarrie's superb cocktails. One to try: the pear-and-pine-accented Dancing Queen. *303 E. Howard Ave., Decatur, GA; 404-378-3502; kimball-house.com.*

Paper Plane

At this neo-retro restaurant-bar with unmarked entrances, Paul Calvert creates distinctive cocktails with uncommon spirits. His Anchor's Away features Wemyss "The Smooth Gentleman" Scotch and Ferreira tawny port. *340 Church St., Decatur, GA; 404-377-9308; the-paper-plane.com.*

MIAMI BEACH

The Broken Shaker

This poolside lounge in the Freehand Miami hostel serves Gui Jaroschy's (p. 32) refreshing cocktails, mixed with homemade syrups, infusions and homegrown and exotic produce. Mel's Gibson (p. 180), for example, includes onion-infused vermouth. *2727 Indian Creek Dr.; 305-531-2727; thefreehand.com.*

The Regent Cocktail Club

With wood accents and a cigar-friendly patio, this retro lounge harks back to the hotel's opening in 1941. Classic cocktails like daiquiris, old-fashioneds and sidecars are served. *1690 Collins Ave.; 305-673-0199; galehotel.com.*

The Rum Line

This Caribbean-inspired outdoor cocktail lounge specializes in rum-centric cocktails, serving 1930s-, '40s- and '50s-style drinks and punches in scorpion bowls. The Cargo Ship, for example, is made with Ron Zacapa 23-year-old rum, Batavia-Arrack, a coffee reduction and mole bitters. *1601 Collins Ave.; 305-695-0110; facebook.com/ TheRumLine.*

NEW ORLEANS

Cane & Table

Housed in a 200-year-old building in the French Quarter, this "rustic Colonial" restaurant and "proto-tiki" bar is from Nick Detrich (p. 30) and Neal Bodenheimer. Cocktails like the Banana Manhattan, a tropical rum variation on the whiskey classic, pay homage to the rum culture of the Caribbean in Colonial days. *1113 Decatur St.; 504-581-1112; caneandtablenola.com.*

Oxalis

The whiskey-focused menu of this Bywater gastropub includes the Nostalgic Old-Fashioned (your choice of any plastic-cap whiskey), the Rosemary Smash (bourbon, dry curaçao, Demerara syrup and lemon) and a selection of boilermakers. *3162 Dauphine St.; 504-267-4776; oxalisbywater.com.*

SoBou

Creole street food is king and Two Bit (25-cent) martinis are on the lunch menu at this restaurant south of Bourbon Street. Head bar chef Abigail Gullo (formerly of NYC's Fort Defiance) creates cocktails like the Charbonneau Way, made with rye whiskey, Suze, maple syrup and fresh thyme. *310 Chartres St.; 504-552-4095; sobounola.com.*

Tiki Tolteca

On the second floor of a French Quarter taqueria, Tiki Tolteca uses homemade liqueurs and syrups in traditional tiki favorites as well as whimsical creations. The menu warns that anyone who drinks the Zombie Punch will turn undead. *301 N. Peters St.; 504-288-8226; felipestaqueria.com.*

DALLAS

Midnight Rambler

This long-awaited cocktail salon is in the basement of the Joule Hotel. The two bars serve shooters, punches and inventive drinks categorized by flavor, such as the aromatic Hocus Pocus, made with ancho chile–infused sherry, tequila, cumin and cacao. *1530 Main St.; 214-261-4601; midnight ramblerbar.com.*

HOUSTON

Captain Foxheart's Bad News Bar & Spirit Lodge

Behind a 25-seat bar with a taxidermied fox, Justin Burrow serves classic cocktails as well as a few original creations. Patrons can enjoy a view of downtown from the large outdoor patio. *308 Main St.; no phone; twitter.com/badnewsbar.*

Julep

Celebrating the cocktail culture of the South, mixologist Alba Huerta (p. 31) specializes in juleps, from the classic bourbon-and-mint version to one with sparkling wine and Cognac. Also on the menu are other twists on classics, like the Armagnac Sazerac. *1919 Washington Ave.; 713-869-4383; julephouston.com.*

AUSTIN

Half Step

Chris Bostick worked for nearly three years to create this cocktail haven with the idea that drinks should be, above all, accessible. Guests choose from two bars: one outdoors with two cocktails on tap and an indoor bar with a menu of five rotating classics. *75½ Rainey St.; 512-391-1877; halfstepbar.com.*

Qui

The team at Qui uses vacuum sealers and sous vide equipment to infuse flavor into the predinner drinks, which are served to every diner. Cocktails offered during the meal are designed to pair with F&W Best New Chef 2014 Paul Qui's globally inspired food. *1600 E. Sixth St.; 512-436-9626; quiaustin.com.*

SAN ANTONIO

Brooklynite

Jeret Pena mans the bar at this sophisticated cocktail parlor done up with vintage furnishings. Pena mixes drinks like the namesake daiquiri and Cereal Milk Punch (made with cereal-infused almond milk) with housemade liqueurs, bitters and juices. *516 Brooklyn Ave.; 210-444-0707; thebrooklynitesa.com.*

Southwest

SCOTTSDALE, ARIZONA

Virtù Honest Craft
Kailee Gielgens is constantly creating new and seasonal cocktails at this restaurant in the Old Town's Bespoke Inn. Recent concoctions include the Virtù Dirty (a dirty martini riff) and the Ice Queen (a vodka cocktail with Champagne foam and black pepper). *3701 N. Marshall Way; 480-946-3477; virtuscottsdale.com.*

LAS VEGAS

Culinary Dropout
This bar in the Hard Rock Hotel & Casino has a relaxed vibe, live music and cocktails organized by category: light and easy, shandies, mules, classics and "Don't Judge Me." The Last Man Standing (Old Overholt rye, pickle and spiced tomato juice in a salt-and-pepper-rimmed glass) falls into that last category. *4455 Paradise Rd.; 702-522-8100; culinarydropout.com.*

West Coast

SAN FRANCISCO

ABV
San Francisco cocktail veterans Ryan Fitzgerald, Erik Reichborn-Kjennerud and Todd Smith run this modern industrial bar. The well-curated cocktail list includes drinks like Lefty's Fizz, with mezcal, grapefruit shrub, dry curaçao and lime. *3174 16th St.; 415-400-4748; abvsf.com.*

Bar5 at Coqueta
The bar at this waterside restaurant specializes in Spanish-style cocktails. These include sherry-based concoctions (like the Andalucía, with walnut liqueur, vinegar, Manchego and golden raisins) and drinks for sharing, served in traditional Spanish pitchers. *Pier 5, Embarcadero Drive; 415-704-8866; coquetasf.com.*

Dirty Habit
This restaurant and lounge occupies the former Fifth Floor space at Hotel Palomar. Brian Means mixes cocktails with brown spirits and old whiskeys in gorgeous antique glassware. *12 Fourth St.; 415-348-1555; dirtyhabitsf.com.*

Trick Dog
At this Mission District bar, the menu is redesigned twice a year; it currently has a Chinese takeout menu theme. Order drink number nine, for instance, and Caitlin Laman (p. 32) will create Nuts for You: bonded bourbon, kumquat cordial and walnut-infused Fernet-Branca. *3010 20th St.; 415-471-2999; trickdogbar.com.*

Trou Normand
A spin-off of the outstanding Bar Agricole, Thad Vogler's new venture is open all day, with a serious food menu. The name refers to the French tradition of cleansing the palate between courses with brandy, hence the focus on digestive spirits like Cognac. *140 New Montgomery St.; 415-975-0876; trounormandsf.com.*

LOS ANGELES AREA

Brilliantshine
The dishes at Brilliantshine were created to complement superstar mixologist Julian Cox's drinks rather than the other way around. Selections from the vast whiskey list appear in cocktails like Ana y Los Lobos, made with 100-proof rye, Cynar, Fernet-Branca and lemon bitters. *522 Wilshire Blvd., Santa Monica; 310-451-0045; thebrilliantshine.com.*

TROU NORMAND
SAN FRANCISCO

The Chestnut Club

The elaborate drinks at this dimly lit, industrial-chic lounge are supplemented by Spanish-style gin-and-tonic variations. The house specialty is the Chestnut Cup, made with gin, Campari, lemon, orgeat and bitters. *1348 14th St., Santa Monica; 310-393-1348; thechestnutclubsm.com.*

Grandpa Johnson's

A 1920s Hollywood Art Deco–inspired design provides the backdrop for innovative drinks made with unusual ingredients. The Lorraine, for example, includes aloe liqueur, pisco, ruby port and rose water. *1638 N. Cahuenga Blvd., Hollywood; 323-467-7300; no website.*

Harlowe

Harlowe's vintage fixtures and classic cocktails are reminiscent of bars from Hollywood's golden age. Star mixologist Dushan Zaric of Employees Only in New York City designed the cocktail program, which includes drinks like the tequila-and-Chartreuse-based Yellow Jacket. *7321 Santa Monica Blvd., West Hollywood; 323-876-5839; harlowebar.com.*

Honeycut

This cavernous basement nightclub in the O Hotel proves that drinks need not be an afterthought at dance venues. You'll find whimsical cocktails like the Juice Box, made with rum, Old Tom gin and lime over fruit punch ice. *819 S. Flower St., L.A.; 213-688-0888; honeycutla.com.*

No Vacancy

Craft cocktails, burlesque shows and live music create the Old Hollywood vibe of this posh bar. A dozen mixologists curate the drinks list, with contributions like The Professor: gin, blood orange liqueur, Aperol and fig bitters. *1727 N. Hudson Ave., L.A.; 323-465-1902; novacancyla.com.*

Sassafras Saloon

This reconstructed Savannah townhouse with quirky Southern artifacts might make you forget you're in the center of downtown Hollywood. Karen Grill (p. 31) specializes in bottled cocktails mixed with homemade preserves. Her tequila-based Garden District includes tomato jam with ancho chile liqueur and lime. *1233 Vine St., L.A.; 323-467-2800; sassafrashollywood.com.*

SAN DIEGO

Polite Provisions

Mixologist Erick Castro is behind the bar program at this reinvention of a 1950s drugstore hangout. More than 40 taps dispense beer, craft sodas and cocktails like the Casual Encounter (gin, organic strawberries and house-made rose petal soda). *4696 30th St.; 619-677-3784; politeprovisions.com.*

PORTLAND, OREGON

Ava Gene's
The carefully curated cocktail list has just nine drinks that showcase aperitivos and digestivos: The Spritz, for instance, combines Prosecco and soda with your choice of Aperol, Campari or Cynar. *3377 SE Division St.; 971-229-0571; avagenes.com.*

Expatriate
Kyle Linden Webster displays the liquors for his signature cocktails at his dramatically lit bar (pictured on p. 204). Naomi Pomeroy, an F&W Best New Chef 2009 (and Webster's wife), designed the snacks menu. *5424 NE 30th Ave.; no phone; expatriatepdx.com.*

Multnomah Whiskey Library
Bartenders climb brass ladders to grab liquors from shelves holding more than 1,500 bottles. The staff helps patrons navigate the inventory via cocktails made tableside, spirits tastings and pairing dinners. *1124 SW Alder St.; 503-954-1381; multnomah whiskeylibrary.com.*

Pépé le Moko
Star mixologist Jeffrey Morgenthaler opened this basement bar beneath his flagship, Clyde Common. Here, he takes much-maligned cocktails like flavored martinis, Long Island Iced Tea and Amaretto Sours and gives them ingenious upgrades. *407 SW 10th Ave.; 503-546-8537; pepelemokopdx.com.*

Raven & Rose
Inspired by the 1883 building that houses Raven & Rose, many of bar director David Shenaut's concoctions are complex and Victorian-themed, like the frothy Absinthe Frappe. Others are bright and fresh. The Improved Cape Codder adds Jacobsen sea salt and Campari to the usual vodka and cranberry juice. *1331 SW Broadway; 503-222-7673; ravenandrosepdx.com.*

St. Jack
Created as a tribute to cafés in Lyon, St. Jack serves French-inspired cocktails. The Savoie Spritz, for example, is made with Dolin blanc vermouth and Génépy, both produced in the Savoie region of France. *1610 NW 23rd Ave.; 503-360-1281; stjackpdx.com.*

SEATTLE AREA

Bar Code
In an upscale pub known for its reinvention of the gin and tonic, bar manager Evan Martin makes his riff on the classic with lime, lemongrass and spices. *1020 108th Ave. NE, Bellevue, WA; 425-455-4278; barcodebellevue.com.*

Damn the Weather
This Pioneer Square restaurant and bar is housed in a century-old building with exposed brick and a shimmering 25-foot white oak bar. The house cocktail, The Woodwork, is dedicated to the company that built the bar and tabletops; it combines orange curaçao and rye whiskey, which is traditionally aged in oak barrels. *116 First Ave. S., Seattle; 206-946-1283; damntheweather.com.*

Percy's and Co.
At this apothecary-style bar, Kyle Taylor and Joe Petersen serve inventive cocktails using infused spirits, fresh fruit and tinctures. The Sankey Sour includes bourbon, Aperol, orange juice and house-made sour mix. *5233 Ballard Ave. NW, Seattle; 206-420-3750; percysseattle.com.*

Radiator Whiskey
This restaurant and bar in the heart of Seattle's Pike Place Market has an impressive assortment of spirits, with the emphasis on whiskeys. The drinks list offers five Manhattan variations as well as strong, bitter cocktails to pair with the kitchen's rich meat dishes. *94 Pike St., Seattle; 206-467-4268; radiatorwhiskey.com.*

Rumba
Serving more than 250 rums, all displayed behind the bar, this rum-centric spot specializes in tiki cocktails, punches and other island drinks. The list includes Caribbean classics like the Queen's Park Swizzle and original daiquiris like the Presidente, made with rum, curaçao, grenadine and vermouth. *1112 Pike St., Seattle; 206-583-7177; rumbaonpike.com.*

Stoneburner
The fixtures in this Italian-accented restaurant and bar in the Hotel Ballard were sourced from a Buenos Aires embassy, a tank factory in upstate New York and the old *New York Times* building. Innovative cocktails include the gin-and-Cognac-based Norfolk Punch: fino sherry, raspberry gum and Boker's bitters. *5214 Ballard Ave. NW, Seattle; 206-695-2051; stoneburnerseattle.com.*

Witness
A bar outfitted with pews and church windows, Witness serves Southern-inspired cocktails like Son of a Preacher Man, with bourbon, black tea, lemon and honey liqueur. *410 Broadway E., Seattle; 206-329-0248; witnessbar.com.*

TACOMA, WASHINGTON

Hilltop Kitchen
The menu at this neighborhood bar focuses on Latin American spirits like mezcal, tequila, rum and cachaça. Half of the drinks are in the "Goes Down Easy" section, like the Banana Daiquiri; the other half are "Boozy & Odd," including the spicy, fruity and smoky Necessity Is a Mother. *913 Martin Luther King Jr. Way; 253-327-1397; hilltopkitchen.com.*

SPOKANE, WASHINGTON

Clover
The drinks from cocktail mastermind Paul Harrington fall into six categories: seasonal, crisp, exuberant, effervescent, spirited and current. In the seasonal camp is the pear gin collins, made with rosemary from the restaurant's on-site greenhouse. *913 E. Sharp Ave.; 509-487-2937; cloverspokane.com.*

Rocky Mountains

DENVER

Ste. Ellie
Located in the basement of the Colt & Gray restaurant, this speakeasy serves uncommon classics such as Air Mails alongside quirky house inventions like the Sherry Sherry Daq Daq, a mix of manzanilla sherry, Drambuie, lime and sage-scented honey syrup. *1553 Platte St.; 303-477-1447; saintellie.com.*

ASPEN

Jimmy's Bodega
This mezcaleria and seafood restaurant is an offshoot of Jimmy's, the beloved restaurant and tequila mecca also in Aspen. Cocktails sold by the bottle include the Vida Buena (mezcal, Aperol and Carpano Antica) and the Puerto de Aspen (blanco tequila, watermelon and lime). *307 S. Mill St.; 970-710-2182; jimmysbodega.com.*

RECIPE INDEX

*Page numbers in **bold** indicate photographs.*

V

W

PHOTO CREDITS

Bar Lexicon

Courtesy of Haus Alpenz (Batavia-Arrack van Oosten, Génépy des Alpes, Zucca; p. 22, 23, 25); PM Spirits (Pineau des Charentes, p. 24); Shaw-Ross (Strega, p. 25)

Mixologist Headshots

Sonya Yu (Chad Arnholt, p. 28); Terry Manier (Ryan Casey, p. 29); Kevin O'Mara (Nick Detrich, p. 30), Anu Apte (Chris Elford, p. 30); Nick Brown (Karen Fu, p. 31); Eugene Lee (Karen Grill, p. 31); Alex Jump (Colin O'Neill, p. 34); Jacqui Krawczyk Segura (Shannon Ponche, p. 34); Nigel Walsh (Tina Ross, p. 35); Paul Wagtouicz (Pamela Wiznitzer, p. 36)

THANK YOU

Jim Meehan
Paul and Victoria deBary
Michael Remaley

CONVERSION CHART

Measures for spirits and other liquids are given in fluid ounces.
Refer to the chart below for conversions.

CUP		OUNCE		TBSP		TSP
1 c	=	8 fl oz				
¾ c	=	6 fl oz				
⅔ c	=	5⅓ fl oz				
		5 fl oz	=	10 tbsp		
½ c	=	4 fl oz				
		3 fl oz	=	6 tbsp		
⅓ c	=	2⅔ fl oz				
¼ c	=	2 fl oz				
		1 fl oz	=	2 tbsp		
		½ fl oz	=	1 tbsp	=	3 tsp
		⅓ fl oz	=	⅔ tbsp	=	2 tsp
		¼ fl oz	=	½ tbsp	=	1½ tsp

1 ounce = about 32 dashes
1 dash = 4 to 5 drops

More books from

FOOD&WINE

ANNUAL COOKBOOK
An entire year of FOOD & WINE recipes.

BEST OF THE BEST
The best recipes from the 25 best cookbooks of the year.

WINE GUIDE
Pocket-size guide with more than 1,000 recommendations.